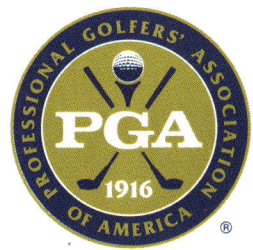

CHAMPIONSHIPS ANNUAL 1997

Writers
Tim Rosaforte
Ron Sirak
Leonard Shapiro
Bill Kwon

Photographers
Michael Cohen
David Cannon
Rusty Jarrett
Craig Jones
Ross Kinnaird
Andy Lyons
Andrew Redington
Jamie Squire

Editor
Bev Norwood

Presented by

The Official Timepiece of
THE PGA OF AMERICA

ISBN 1-878843-21-4
©1997 PGA of America
100 Avenue of The Champions
Palm Beach Gardens, Florida 33410

Published by International Merchandising Corporation
One Erieview Plaza
Cleveland, Ohio 44114

Designed and produced by Davis Design

Course illustrations courtesy of NYT Special Services, Inc.,
Ryder Cup Ltd. Publishing, and Poipu Bay Resort.

Printed in the United States of America

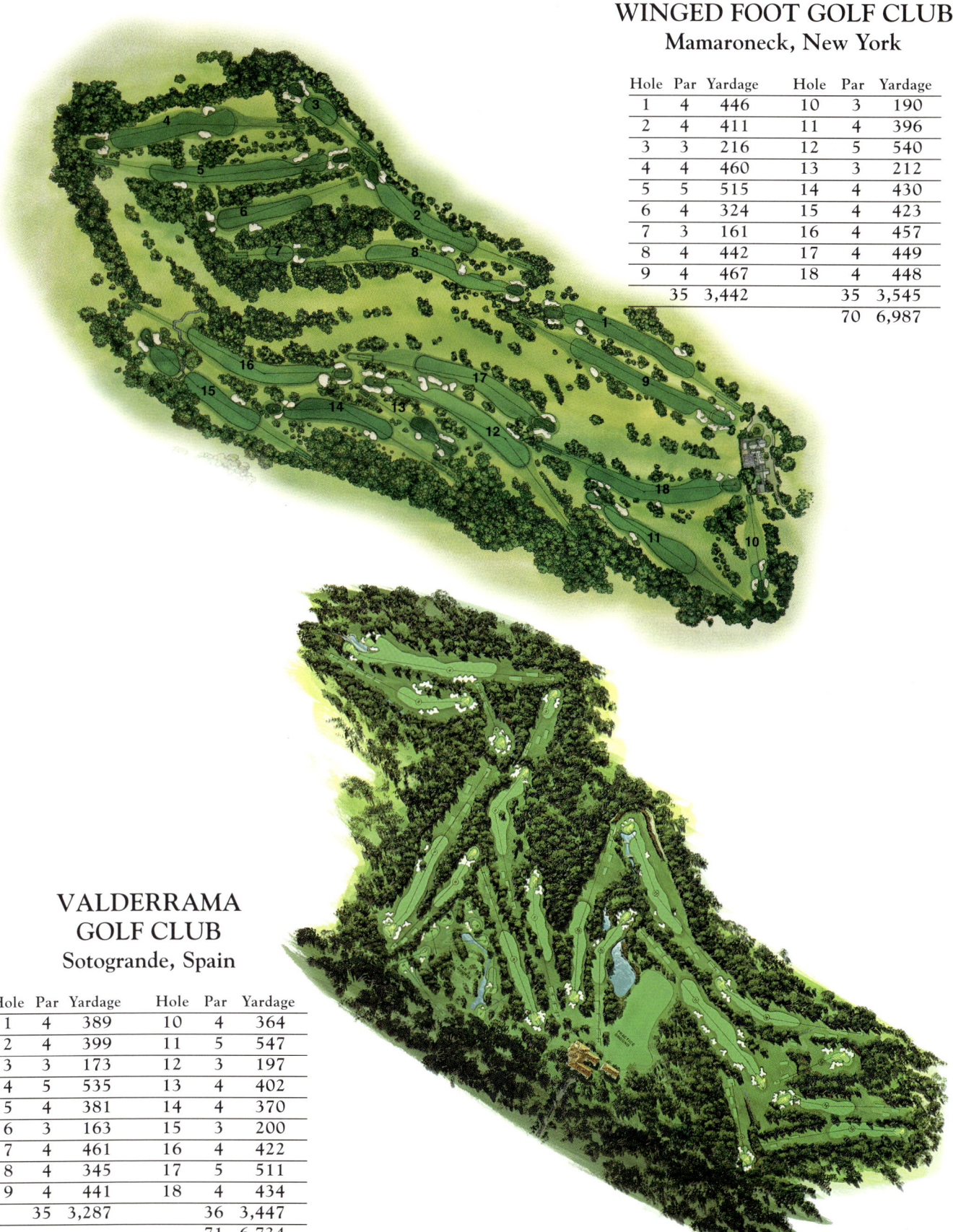

WINGED FOOT GOLF CLUB
Mamaroneck, New York

Hole	Par	Yardage	Hole	Par	Yardage
1	4	446	10	3	190
2	4	411	11	4	396
3	3	216	12	5	540
4	4	460	13	3	212
5	5	515	14	4	430
6	4	324	15	4	423
7	3	161	16	4	457
8	4	442	17	4	449
9	4	467	18	4	448
	35	3,442		35	3,545
				70	6,987

VALDERRAMA GOLF CLUB
Sotogrande, Spain

Hole	Par	Yardage	Hole	Par	Yardage
1	4	389	10	4	364
2	4	399	11	5	547
3	3	173	12	3	197
4	5	535	13	4	402
5	4	381	14	4	370
6	3	163	15	3	200
7	4	461	16	4	422
8	4	345	17	5	511
9	4	441	18	4	434
	35	3,287		36	3,447
				71	6,734

CHAMPIONSHIPS ANNUAL 1997

	Page
58th PGA Seniors' Championship	10
79th PGA Championship	30
32nd Ryder Cup Matches	62
MasterCard PGA Grand Slam	82

FOREWORD

One of the greatest and newest thrills in my life is to examine the list of PGA Champions and competitors who have come before me: Raymond Floyd, who, like me, is the son of a PGA Professional; Jack Nicklaus, who was my boyhood hero; Arnold Palmer, who was my father's adulthood hero; Snead and Nelson and Hogan, a holy trinity for the ages; Paul Runyan, who won in 1934, an old friend of my father's and now an old friend of mine. It is a privilege and an honor to be among that group.

This book, the *PGA Championships Annual* for 1997, will have a prominent place on my bookshelf, right alongside Harvey Penick's books. It illustrates beautifully, in words and pictures, what I was able to accomplish over four wonderful days in August of 1997 on that splendid treachery called Winged Foot. There's good golf on every page of this book, by Tour players, by Senior players, by club professionals and by internationals. Golf is not only the game for a lifetime, it is also a game for people throughout the world.

Winged Foot is a special place. The PGA Championship is a special event. My win, my first major, means more to me than any professional victory. I will always cherish the moment shared with friends and family. Thanks to the PGA of America for making it all possible.

Davis Love III

PGA CHAMPIONSHIPS ANNUAL 1997

Hale Irwin, winner of 58th PGA Seniors' Championship.

Davis Love III, winner of 79th PGA Championship.

The European Team, winner of the 32nd Ryder Cup Matches.

Ernie Els, winner of MasterCard PGA Grand Slam.

IRWIN TAKES OLD APPROACH, SECOND TITLE

By Tim Rosaforte

On Wednesday evening, the night before the opening round of the PGA Seniors' Championship, Hale Irwin was in the Health and Racquet Club at the PGA National Resort and Spa in Palm Beach Gardens, Florida. He spent two hours pumping iron, stretching, and doing his cardiovascular work, before taking his wife, Sally, to dinner at a popular nearby restaurant called Cafe Chardonnay. He did this Thursday night, Friday night and Saturday night, too, because this was the routine he followed in 1996, when he won the PGA Seniors' by two strokes, and while Irwin isn't superstitious, he is dedicated.

The 1996 PGA Seniors' Championship was Irwin's first major championship on the Senior PGA Tour, and figured to be the first of many for the three-time U.S. Open Champion. Instead, it was the last win of any kind for the year. He would finish second seven times, including runner-up finishes in the U.S. Senior Open and the Senior Players Championship. Financially, it added up to the most lucrative season in his golf career — he was the fastest player in Senior Tour history to reach $1 million in earnings, taking just 13

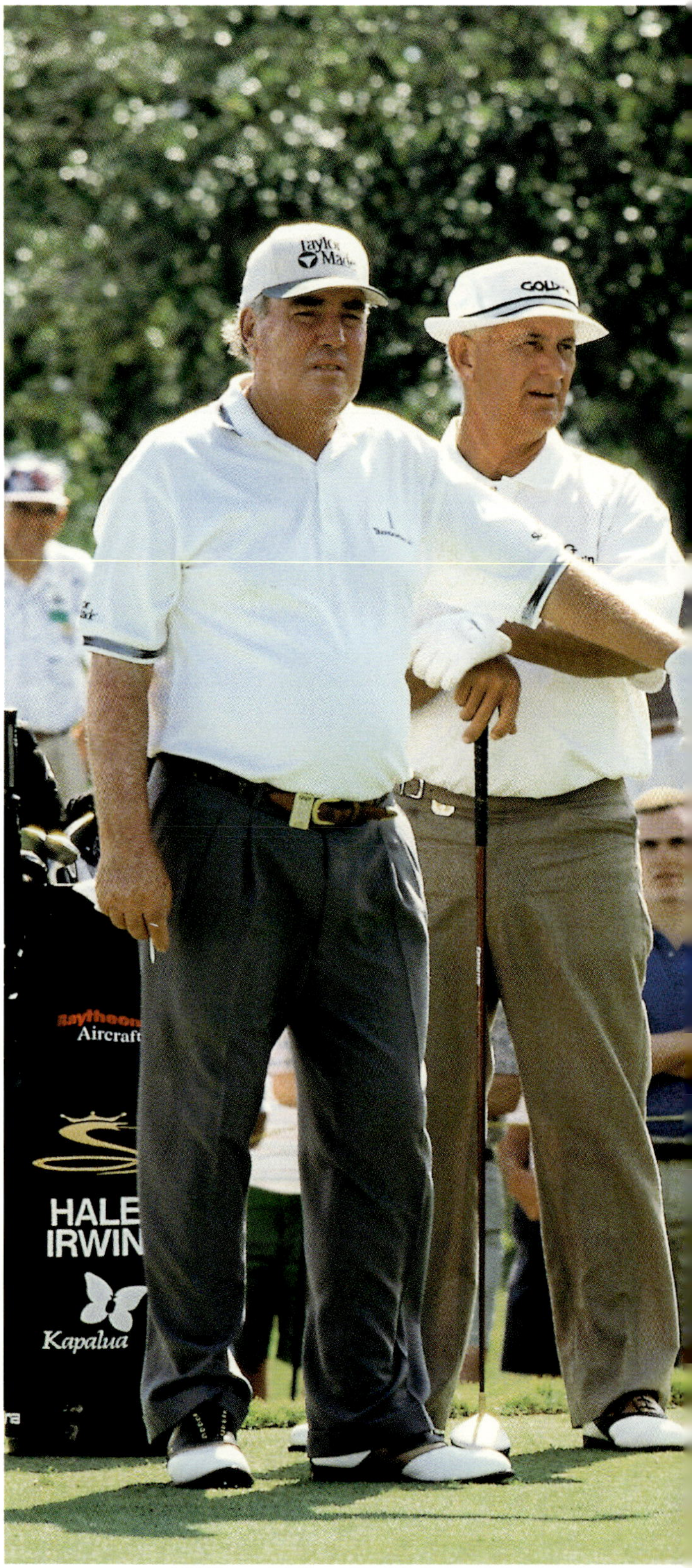

As John Bland and Larry Gilbert (left) came to see, Hale Irwin

combined patience with his skill and experience to become a dominant player on the Senior PGA Tour in 1997.

Leading by seven strokes after 36 and 54 holes, Irwin dominated the 58th PGA Seniors' Championship.

events to reach seven figures. In many ways, however, it was the most frustrating season in the 28 years Hale Irwin had spent playing professional golf.

It didn't really bother him that Jim Colbert won the money title on the last hole in 1996, or that Colbert edged him out for Player of the Year honors. The man may have played in nine more events, but he did win five times and he deserved the post-season awards.

What Irwin didn't like was his own inability to finish golf tournaments. You don't win three U.S. Opens and 17 other events on the PGA Tour without being able to close on Sunday. Hale Irwin didn't suddenly forget how to do that overnight.

So he went back into his own memory bank during the holidays and replayed the tapes of those seven tournaments where he was a runner-up. He compared his mistakes and the bounces he got in the losses to the decisions he made and the shots he hit at the PGA Seniors' Championship. He thought back to the Opens at Winged Foot and Inverness, where the winning score was over par, and to Medinah, where he shot 65 on Sunday and won the Monday playoff against Mike Donald.

It all came back to him. He realized that instead of worrying about winning on the first day or the second day, he would be more patient. Then he would let his strength and conditioning and experience in major championships take over. "There were at least two or three events last year where I think I really just packaged it up and gave it away," Irwin said. "And that's unlike me. So I just kind of thought over the Christmas holidays, what could I do this year to really improve myself? Well, I wanted to win. Winning, as I go back, that is the number one thing. But how could I do it? I did go out and hit some more balls. I did change my irons from Cobra to Cobra ... the newest clubs. And they worked great. But more than anything, it's an approach."

The new approach — or the old approach — paid off early in 1997 with victories at the MasterCard Championship, the LG Championship and the Senior Slam. Rather than pushing the envelope, he was picking his spots. At the MasterCard Championship, for example, he outdueled Gil Morgan on the back nine at the Haulalai Golf Club in Kailua-Kona, Hawaii. Two weeks later, at Bay Colony Golf Club in Naples, Florida, he shot 65 in the final round and passed Bob Murphy for a one-stroke victory. With two victories in two tournaments, the plan he put into place was working quite nicely.

"There were times last year when I think I tried to put the slipper on the wrong foot. It's just the club, the shot, that I was trying to play that just didn't fit the time, just didn't fit the scene. It wasn't what I should have done. Consequently, I tried to take a step back and look at it differently. Maybe look at it from the side, and maybe that's not the way to play the shot. And really, with the experience I've had, the success I've had, I can go down the stretch and compete. But I don't try to win it at the 14th or the 15th hole. You're not going to win it on the first tee. Most of these tournaments are going to be won and lost on the latter few holes. So just keep hanging in there and do the smart thing. That's what I'm trying to do sometimes, not put the pedal to the metal, just coast in there sometimes."

When it came down to Sunday in the 58th PGA Seniors' Championship, Irwin had built up such a lead that in the press room he was being compared to Tiger Woods. With Irwin seven shots up after 36 holes and 54 holes, the story lines between Tiger's runaway victory in the Masters Tournament the week before and Irwin's march to his second consecutive PGA Seniors' Championship title had become blurred. It finally reached a point where Irwin started suggesting nicknames for himself. "Are we going to call me 'Pussycat?' " he said. "Or how about, 'The Cub?' "

In relative terms, Irwin still was a cub. In fact,

Gibby Gilbert's opening 69 led to a fourth-place tie.

Dale Douglass shared second despite a 76.

Jack Nicklaus was saying, "We've got to get him out of diapers and make him understand who he is." But a pussycat? Hardly. When it came to intensity, Hale Irwin was competitive with anyone who's ever put on a pair of golf spikes. You don't play the safety position in the Big Eight, as Irwin did for Colorado, and not take a little of that football mentality with you to the golf course.

Irwin's problem, early in his Senior PGA Tour career, was that he still felt competitive on the regular tour. Rather than focusing on just one circuit, he tried to play both tours, and as Raymond Floyd proved, that just doesn't work. As Floyd and Irwin found, there's plenty of competition going against the graybeards on the Senior PGA Tour every week.

The previous year, Irwin competed in The Players Championship, the Tradition and the Masters, in the weeks leading up to the PGA Seniors' Championship. In 1997, he spent the week before the tournament making trips to three golf courses that he was designing in Prescott, Arizona; Wichita, Kansas, and Tunica, Mississippi. He also spent several days relaxing with his wife in High Point, North Carolina, and at their home in St. Louis, before arriving in Palm Beach Gardens.

"Hale's now getting comfortable with the senior circuit," Colbert said. "He's got the mindset to show everybody how good he is. He doesn't want to play Tiger and the rest of the guys anymore."

On Sunday, even when he was trying to play conservatively, Irwin found the hole kept getting in the way of the ball. He shot a cruise-control 68 to win by 12 strokes, which was the same margin of victory Tiger enjoyed at Augusta National. It was the largest winning margin in the history of the Senior PGA Tour, and it made him the first back-to-back winner of the PGA Seniors' Championship since Sam Snead triumphed in 1972 and 1973.

That he won again at PGA National was not

John Schroeder started with 70, his only sub-par round.

surprising. The Champion course at PGA National Golf Club has a reputation for being one of the most feared on the Senior PGA Tour. Four of its holes made the top 18 as the toughest on the Senior PGA Tour in 1996, and two more were in the top 50. This is not a driver-wedge layout. This is a track that hosted a PGA Championship and a Ryder Cup in the 1980s, and even though Jack Nicklaus redesigned it, he didn't take the teeth out of it. "It likes me and I like it and we have a mutual respect," Irwin said.

Following his game plan of being patient and letting the tournament come to him, Irwin had positioned himself right where he wanted to be after the opening round. At three-under-par 69, he trailed John Bland of South Africa by two strokes, and was one of three golfers in the 144-man field to break 70. Bland was at 67, followed by Irwin and Gibby Gilbert at 68, with Dale Douglass, John Schroeder, Isao Aoki, Gary Player and Gil Morgan at 70. Morgan, who had shot 22 under par to win the Tradition, was the new kid on the block, so to speak, turning 50 the previous September.

John Bland led the first round with 67, then shot 77.

Bland had been around for one year longer than Morgan, and had made the most of it, winning five times in 20 months and making over $1.6 million. With 20 victories around the world, he was quite capable of holding on and winning the PGA Seniors' Championship. As a Monday qualifier, he won the Ralph's Senior Classic, and that was his ticket to a Senior PGA Tour exemption. In 1996, he won four times, earned over $1.3 million and was named Rookie of the Year. So while it was easy to write him off as being "Bland," he could play, and on Thursday at the Champion course, he did.

The highlight of his round was an eagle two he made at the 395-yard ninth, when his six-iron shot from 165 yards found the cup. He had started with a birdie at the first from the fairway bunker, and then, after a bogey at the second, got back to one under par with a pitch shot to four feet at the third. But it was that six iron at the ninth that got him going, and he birdied the 10th, 11th and 16th holes to go to six under. He dropped a shot at the 17th, and failed to birdie the par-five 18th, but still, it was the best score posted by two shots and one of only three scores in the 60s.

The difference, of course, was the eagle at the ninth. "It was always on line and the next thing, there it was," Bland said. "Those things don't happen very often, so I had the right yardage anyway. It's not anything that happens very often, but it's nice when it does happen anyway."

Bland had a decided advantage by teeing off at 8 a.m. It had rained hard on Wednesday, and the course, at 6,722 yards, was playing long. By Thursday afternoon, when the wind picked up, the course played even longer. As Bob Charles said, "Bland played early, while the tide was still in." Indeed, of the 25 players who shot par or better, only eight came in the afternoon, but those are the breaks of the game.

The PGA of America did not give the players lift, clean and place relief, but there was casual water and Bland chose to take six drops. Even though balls were plugging in the fairway and balls were caking up with mud, it was the same for everybody. "This is a major championship, and the Rules of Golf apply," said Kerry Haigh, the PGA's Senior Director of Tournaments. "The Rules of Golf state you should play the ball as it lies."

The dicey part was determining casual water. Gibby Gilbert, who was tied with Irwin in second place at 69, had 118 yards into the green at the 18th hole, and although there was no visible water, he knew his wedge would hit some taking a divot. "I really hit a good shot, and it squirted," he said. "When I hit it, water splattered all over the place and I hit it just off the back of the green."

Gary Player, a three-time PGA Seniors' Champion, applauded the PGA's decision. "It seems like every time we have a little bit of rain, and there is a little speck of mud on the ball, some players scream, 'Lift, clean and place,'" Player said. "I like it when we don't touch the ball. We play the golf course and play the game."

Irwin, who made four birdies, is such a purist, he deliberately did not take one casual water drop. "The under-foot stuff was just wet," he said. "I don't think it affected play as much as the above-ground stuff. To me, the wind here is more of a factor than playing with damp conditions. It's no worse than if you had heavy dew."

At the third hole, Irwin's tee shot picked up enough mud that it looked like a chocolate cupcake. He hit wedge from 84 yards to four feet, and made the putt for birdie. "Boy, there was Terra Sloppa on my ball," he said. "I mean, [the mud] was probably a third the size of a golf ball. Had it been a full shot, I don't know where it was going to go. But that's OK. To me, that's the game. That's why we play here, because not everything is predictable. Not everything is the way in your mind you want it. You have to deal with some adversity. I prefer to do it that way."

No one had faced more adversity in recent months than Arnold Palmer. Diagnosed for prostate cancer in January, he had come back to play

Arnold Palmer returned after prostate surgery.

the opening round of his Bay Hill Invitational in March, and was at Augusta for the first two rounds of the Masters. In the PGA Seniors' Championship, a tournament he won in 1980 and 1984, Palmer went out in 37, but tired on the back nine. At the 12th, he shanked two irons from a fairway bunker out of bounds and made nine. At the par-three 17th, he hit into the water and made triple bogey. Coming home in 47, Palmer shot 84, but gave a lesson in handling adversity. As playing companion Gil Morgan said, "Arnie didn't play well, but he didn't let his disappointment carry over and cause you to feel upset or anything like that. Some people get upset and moody, but he isn't like that."

Palmer admitted he never recovered after three-putting the 10th from a short distance. "It's starting to get better and I feel a little better about it," he said. "But when you make a couple of mistakes, you get tired. It's a combination of being a little tired and losing your enthusiasm. I'll get over

Despite a painful hip, Jack Nicklaus shared second place with rounds of 71, 72, 73 and 70.

it, and tomorrow, we'll give it another try."

In the group at 71 was Nicklaus. On Wednesday, complaining of hip pain, he had to withdraw after nine holes from a practice round with Palmer and Player. Nicklaus looked in so much pain that Palmer suggested he get the hip treated. Nicklaus sort of bristled. "What am I going to do? Go to Ace Hardware?" he said. "I'll figure out what I'm going to do when the time comes."

When it was time to count scores, Nicklaus gutted out one of 14 sub-par rounds. His 71 was also six strokes better than his opening-round 77 in 1996. "When a tournament starts, my body will cooperate to whatever degree it will cooperate," he said. "I've been hurting and I'm going to continue to hurt. That's not a big deal. The big deal is I'm having trouble getting the ball in the hole."

Irwin didn't have that trouble on Friday. He made six birdies and holed out from a fairway bunker at the 13th for an eagle to take that seven-stroke lead over Bob Charles. His only bogey occurred when he hit the wrong club over the ninth green, and had Charles not birdied the 18th, Irwin would have tied a PGA Seniors' and PGA Tour record for a 36-hole lead. "Darn," Irwin said jokingly. "You cannot depend on 'Lefty.' He just always screws things up."

When Irwin won the PGA Seniors' Championship in 1996, he opened with 66, slipped on Friday to 74, came back on Saturday with 69, and then played conservatively on Sunday, shooting 71. He was able to finish bogey-bogey and still win by two strokes over Isao Aoki. The sequence in 1997 was decidedly different. Irwin's second-round 65 was one of only three rounds in the 60s. Larry Gilbert shot 69 to move from 42nd to fourth place, and Bud Allin, the Vietnam vet who finished tied for fourth at PGA National in 1996, also shot 69 after an opening-round 76.

Bland ballooned 10 strokes higher to 77 and had dropped into a tie for eighth with his playing companion, Ch Chi Rodriguez, who had started the day in 41st place but was able to move 33 spots up the leaderboard by shooting 74. In cool and breezy conditions, the stroke average for the field was 77.21, which was nearly one stroke higher than Thursday's average.

Coming off a birdie at the 15th, Bland got stuck in the second and third legs of the Bear Trap. At No. 16, he was just off the green in two shots, but his ball was in a divot and he bladed a chip into three-putt land. Double bogey. The par-three 17th was the fifth toughest hole on the Senior PGA Tour in 1996. Bland added to its reputation. His tee shot plugged in a bunker, and from that lie, he flew the green into the water. Another double bogey, his third of the day. It can happen quickly in the Bear Trap, and it did for Bland. "I didn't hit a bad shot off the tee or anything like that," he said. "It's really very tricky."

Rodriguez would call it deadly. "Those holes remind me of Dr. Kevorkian," he said. "And I don't want to see him."

Gibby Gilbert also had three double bogeys, but shot 73 and was alone in third place at two-under-par 142. "Three bad swings," he said. "Normally you have to pay to ride a roller coaster like I was on today. It's unbelievable."

At the second, he drove 50 yards right of where he was aiming, almost out of bounds. From the trees, Gilbert pitched back to the fairway, and from 149 yards, left a six iron short and in the fringe. A good chip could have saved bogey, but he ran it 12 feet past and two-putted.

At the sixth, the wind was blowing left to right, so Gilbert figured he could draw a tee shot into it. Instead, he duck-hooked his drive into the water, 40 yards left of where he was aiming. His ball never crossed land, so he had to re-tee and made par on his second ball.

At the 16th, after battling back with his fourth birdie at No. 15, Gilbert made his third bad swing of the day. This tee shot was not a push like No. 2, or a duck hook like No. 6; this was more of a fan-tail slice. It ended up in the fairway bunker, and he compounded the bad tee shot by hitting an

Bob Charles was second with his 71-70 start.

Irwin's 65 in the second round opened a seven-shot lead.

Larry Gilbert was the closest challenger after 54 holes.

iron thin, and into the water hazard. He had to make a six-footer just to make a double bogey.

Gilbert had been struggling with his health since winning the Royal Caribbean Classic in January. He finished 10th the following week in Naples, and in Tampa for the GTE Suncoast Classic, tore the paraphoras muscle in his hip and had to withdraw. He missed four weeks, actually came back two weeks too early, and had to revert to his old swing. His new one, taught by Jim McLean the previous December at the Diners Club Matches, involved restricting hip turn on the back swing, and accelerating it on the downswing.

"You can't teach old muscles a new swing," he said.

On the subject of old muscles, Palmer continued to struggle, shooting 82 to miss the cut, and Nicklaus, still limping, battled through two double bogeys to shoot 72 in semi-touch with Irwin. He was at 143, one of only nine golfers under par at the midway point, and if Irwin wasn't in the tournament, Nicklaus would have only been two strokes off the lead held by Charles. But already, it was shaping up into a battle for second place. Hale Irwin had turned it into a one-man tournament.

"I think what you have is a lot of old guys playing golf," he said. "If we were real sharp, we wouldn't be playing on this tour, we'd be playing some other tour. We're seniors. Give us a test that's fairly difficult, where you're going to have to work around the green with touch, then the guys have a little trouble with it, as we all did. The greens were the toughest part of the golf course today, no question about it. And the golf course is also playing fairly long, which is unusual for here. The par-fives are not gimmes this week, and that's another key to what's happening. In previous years, most of the par-fives are able to be reached in two [shots]. The guys would walk off the course and if they're only three under on the par-fives, they were really upset. Not so this

Gil Morgan didn't break par after the first day.

John Morgan shot 72s in the last three rounds.

year. Hale is the only one not having trouble with it."

Irwin was five under on the par-fives through 36 holes, and by comparison, Charles was even par, Gilbert was one over and Nicklaus was one under. Although his driving distance statistics weren't off the charts (partially because the fairways were soft), Irwin was carrying the ball farther than playing companion Dave Stockton could remember. At one point in the second round, Stockton asked Irwin if he was using a new driver. Irwin said it was the same club, and explained why his ball flight and sound at contact was so much better. "It's just timing and getting a good turn and getting it in the hitting position," Irwin said. "I just get a better swing going, and when that works, I'm getting the ball out there a lot farther. Instead of slapping at it, I'm driving it."

As well as he was scoring, Irwin still wasn't secure with his game. He wasn't warming up well, and was getting away with bad swings while the rest of the field wasn't. It went back to the game plan he outlined during Christmas and sticking

Chi Chi Rodriguez was not a contender.

to it. At the 13th hole, he went for a pin he probably shouldn't have and got away with it, knocking wedge into the hole from the sand, 155 yards away. But at the sixth, a par-five hole that he wasn't going to reach anyway, Irwin hit a four wood off the tee, figuring if he was going to lay up anyway, why not lay up twice? It resulted in a birdie, his third straight in a run of four.

His birdie putts were 15, 10, six, 12, seven and four feet. He only took 24 putts, and that eagle didn't hurt his stats. "It was a superior round, but I still didn't play as well as I would have liked," he said. "At the same time, I hit an awful lot of very, very good shots and I putted much better today. I feel like I'm managing my game well and I'm doing the things that are providing opportunities for myself."

Irwin didn't have his "A" game on Saturday, but it didn't really matter. There was one man who could have made it a golf tournament, but once Gibby Gilbert walked off the 11th green, the Fat Lady started warming up her vocal chords.

"This is the type of course you can go along real well for 10 holes, and one hole can ruin the whole week," Gilbert said. "I was just playing. I was not worried about Hale. I was not worried about anything. I was playing well for 10 holes and the bottom dropped out."

Gilbert had trimmed Irwin's seven-shot lead down to three strokes. He started out with three straight birdies, and picked up another stroke with a birdie at the par-five sixth. Irwin birdied the

The crowds followed Irwin throughout his 72 in the third round, his worst score of the week.

Gibby Gilbert's second shot on the 11th ran across the fairway into the rough, leading to a quintuple-bogey nine.

ninth, sticking a nine iron to two inches, to turn in 35, but gave that back with a three-putt bogey at the par-five 10th. Without warning, Irwin's putter had deserted him. "I wasn't feeling any pressure from the outside, in this case, Gibby, let's say," he said. "I felt more frustrated with myself. I could have almost maintained that same pace with him had I been putting anywhere near the way I should have. I was more concerned about my own scoring prowess than his."

Gilbert started the 11th hole by hooking his drive down the left side, nearly in a pond. From the hazard, Gilbert wanted to pitch back into the fairway, where he could hit a shot onto the green and make no worse than bogey. Instead, he hit a shot that ran across the fairway and into the right rough. Now, he was really in trouble.

From there, he had no shot, and again just tried to pitch it back in the fairway. This time he was successful, but he still had 113 yards to the pin, and was playing his fourth shot. This is where it got ugly. A fat wedge came up short and spun back into the hazard. From there, he flew the green into the back bunker. Now, he was lying five. His sixth shot stopped 35 feet from the hole, and when Gilbert left his first putt five feet short, he was looking at a quintuple-bogey nine — which is what he made. Nine strokes, no lost balls, and one devastated golfer.

"I kept trying to play safe to make bogey," Gilbert said. "I thought I was trying the right shot every time. Obviously I wasn't. Then I got in po-

Charles shared seventh with his closing 72.

John Morgan tied for fourth despite this shot.

Larry Gilbert tumbled to 75 in the last round.

Walter Morgan closed with 71 for 10th place.

Douglass had a second-place tie after his final 69.

Jack Kiefer finished well and tied for fourth.

sition where I couldn't make bogey, so I tried to play safe and make double bogey."

Irwin showed no sympathy, knowing the 11th could exact that type of score to anyone in the PGA Seniors' Championship field. Of the 74 players who made the 36-hole cut, 12 made bogey, nine made double bogey, and four, including Gilbert, made triple bogey or higher. With a stroke average of 4.473, it was the hardest hole on the golf course that day, and would prove to be for the tournament. "I was more concerned about my bogey," Irwin said, "than his disaster."

In one hole, Gilbert had given back everything he earned over the first 10. He bogeyed the 12th and 17th holes coming in, but was still able to post a respectable 74. He never lost his temper, and at the end of the day, was tied for fifth place with Morgan, Nicklaus and Charles, 10 strokes back of Irwin. Bland had made a comeback after his second-round 77, and shot 71 to tie for third with John Morgan of Oxford, England, at one-under-par 216.

Morgan had played in the 1995 and 1996 PGA Seniors' Championship, shooting rounds of 84-78 and 77-77 to miss two cuts. But that was part

Nicklaus had a 10-foot birdie putt to share second.

Irwin had a lot to smile about on the last day.

of golf's learning experience. He was fortunate to play a practice round with Nicklaus in 1996, and a year later, ended up paired with Jack for the third round. He shot 72 to Jack's 73, which also earned a final-round pairing.

"I remember playing here with Jack in a practice round last year, and yes, I was shaking like a leaf," Morgan remembered. "I hit a two iron off the first tee and hit it about 160 yards. I'm thinking he's God and I'm nobody. Now, here we are and we're almost even. A lot can happen in a year."

Larry Gilbert had pulled to within five shots of Irwin after the 13th hole, but went bogey-bogey and parred in for 70. At 213, he took over second place. Gilbert had finished second in 1995 at PGA National, and that was the position everybody would be playing for on Sunday.

"Catch Hale?" he said. "Oh, good night."

Gilbert, of course, was right. The only real drama was the battle for second place, and Nicklaus recorded a moral victory by making a 10-foot birdie putt at the last to shoot 70 and tie Douglass for second. Jack Kiefer, Gibby Gilbert and John Morgan tied for fourth, and for Morgan, the $55,000 represented the biggest check of his career.

"We were talking in the second fairway," Nicklaus said, "and he said to me, 'I sure am glad we played that practice round together last year.'"

They were tied going to the 18th. Morgan hit a big drive that had him contemplating eagle. "It would have been very nice to have beaten him," Morgan said. "I'm very disappointed to have taken a six at the last to Jack's birdie."

Nicklaus never likes to finish second, but he took pride in playing as hard as he did with the bad hip in his third straight week of tournament golf. "I always felt it was important to finish the best you can," he said. "People pay money to watch me play. I want to give 100 percent all the time, but, sometimes, I can't get my heart into it. But you have to do the best you can with what

Sally and Hale went home with a second PGA Seniors' Championship.

you have. I guess that's what keeps me playing."

Douglass, who missed the cut in 1996, and who had not finished better than ninth on the Senior PGA Tour in 1997, acknowledge that Irwin was the class of the Senior PGA Tour. "We've got several guys who can play with him," Douglass said. "But he's our best."

Charles, who tied Bland and Larry Gilbert for seventh, agreed. "He's a good iron player and he attacks the hole," Charles said. "He's able to spin the ball and keep it close to the flag. I don't put a lot of spin on the ball, and I'm bouncing and kicking into the flag or past the flag. He's going for the bottom of the flag."

Out on the golf course, Irwin was being called "Tiger Irwin," and he thought to himself, "What is wrong with Hale Woods?" At the 15th tee, a new spin was put on the old mantra, when somebody yelled, "You're the old man!"

Hale Irwin smiled. A year ago on that same tee, trying to protect a four-stroke lead over Aoki, Irwin hit a soft-fading five iron to the left side of the green, let out a mouthful of air, headed to the watercooler, and said to the spectators lining the tee, "I'm getting too old for this."

He came back, older, and wiser, finished birdie-birdie-par-par, collected a check for $216,000, called Cafe Chardonnay for a to-go order, and if he wasn't heading to the airport, Hale Irwin would have caught a quick workout at the PGA Health and Racquet Club, then taken Sally to dinner at the restaurant.

"To be two shots behind after the first round and win by 12 … well, I must've been doing a lot of good things," Irwin said. "I would've hated to be chasing me today."

58th PGA Seniors' Championship

April 17-20, 1997, PGA National Golf Club (Champion Course),
Palm Beach Gardens, Florida

Contestant	Rounds				Total	Prize
Hale Irwin	69	65	72	68	274	$216,000.00
Jack Nicklaus	71	72	73	70	286	105,000.00
Dale Douglass	70	76	71	69	286	105,000.00
John Morgan	71	72	72	72	287	55,000.00
Gibby Gilbert	69	73	74	71	287	55,000.00
Jack Kiefer	72	72	73	70	287	55,000.00
Larry Gilbert	74	69	70	75	288	40,000.00
John Bland	67	77	71	73	288	40,000.00
Bob Charles	71	70	75	72	288	40,000.00
Walter Morgan	74	75	69	71	289	30,000.00
David Graham	75	75	70	70	290	19,625.00
Kermit Zarley	76	75	72	67	290	19,625.00
Tommy Horton	72	76	69	73	290	19,625.00
John Schroeder	70	74	73	73	290	19,625.00
Seiichi Kanai	72	76	74	69	291	15,000.00
DeWitt Weaver	75	74	70	72	291	15,000.00
Dave Stockton	72	76	73	70	291	15,000.00
Bud Allin	76	69	74	72	291	15,000.00
Gil Morgan	70	73	73	75	291	15,000.00
Isao Aoki	70	79	70	73	292	13,000.00
Gary Player	70	77	75	70	292	13,000.00
Graham Marsh	72	75	71	74	292	13,000.00
Bruce Summerhays	72	76	76	69	293	11,500.00
Jerry McGee	76	74	71	72	293	11,500.00
Brian Barnes	76	73	73	71	293	11,500.00
J.C. Snead	73	79	71	71	294	10,500.00
Chi Chi Rodriguez	74	70	75	76	295	9,000.00
Calvin Peete	75	72	73	75	295	9,000.00
Lee Trevino	75	73	72	75	295	9,000.00
Jim Albus	72	78	74	71	295	9,000.00
Bob Murphy	73	72	75	75	295	9,000.00
Jim Colbert	76	73	74	73	296	7,000.00
Jim Jewell	72	74	74	76	296	7,000.00
Gay Brewer	75	75	74	72	296	7,000.00
Vicente Fernandez	73	77	70	77	297	5,000.00
Mike Hill	73	73	74	77	297	5,000.00
Raymond Floyd	75	73	79	70	297	5,000.00
Jose Maria Canizares	73	76	75	73	297	5,000.00
Hugh Baiocchi	77	71	75	74	297	5,000.00
Steve Benson	74	78	72	74	298	3,200.00
Bob Dickson	73	77	72	76	298	3,200.00
Dana Quigley	75	71	75	77	298	3,200.00
Dick Rhyan	74	71	76	77	298	3,200.00
Bob E. Smith	73	76	75	74	298	3,200.00
Jay Sigel	79	72	71	76	298	3,200.00
Frank Conner	75	71	76	77	299	2,458.34
Rick Acton	73	73	76	77	299	2,458.34
Rocky Thompson	72	77	81	69	299	2,458.33
Mike McCullough	73	77	71	78	299	2,458.33
Jimmy Powell	71	77	76	75	299	2,458.33
Larry Mowry	73	72	76	78	299	2,458.33
Terry Gale	78	71	76	75	300	2,125.00

58TH PGA SENIORS' CHAMPIONSHIP

Contestant	Rounds				Total	Prize
Walter Zembriski	74	77	73	76	300	2,125.00
Bill Garrett	73	77	73	77	300	2,125.00
Charles Coody	73	76	73	78	300	2,125.00
Bill King	76	74	77	74	301	2,000.00
Bill Hall	77	74	76	75	302	1,925.00
Ed Everett	73	79	73	77	302	1,925.00
Randy Glover	77	74	77	75	303	1,781.25
Miller Barber	71	74	82	76	303	1,781.25
Antonio Garrido	74	76	76	77	303	1,781.25
Dick Goetz	76	73	79	75	303	1,781.25
Tom Shaw	75	73	81	75	304	1,687.50
Charlie Epps	75	75	78	76	304	1,687.50
Michael DiBuono	75	76	76	78	305	1,637.50
Martin Roesink	78	74	79	74	305	1,637.50
Malcolm Gregson	73	79	76	79	307	1,575.00
Bill Miller	78	74	75	80	307	1,575.00
Bruce Crampton	78	72	82	75	307	1,575.00
Bill Kennedy	78	73	85	74	310	1,525.00
Roger Kennedy	74	77	82	79	312	1,487.50
Jon Cutshall	77	74	75	86	312	1,487.50
Bob Thatcher	77	75	85	76	313	1,450.00
Bunky Henry	73	78	82	82	315	1,425.00

Out of Final 36 Holes

Contestant	R1	R2	Total	Contestant	R1	R2	Total
Marty Bohen	71	82	153	Noel Ratcliffe	77	81	158
Lou Graham	75	78	153	Bob Leaver	75	83	158
Hubert Green	75	78	153	Bob Irving	80	79	159
Terry Dill	76	77	153	John Rech	81	78	159
Dan Wood	77	76	153	Fred Hawkins	80	79	159
Mitoshi Tomita	76	77	153	Wes Smith	74	85	159
Joe Jimenez	76	77	153	Bud Williamson	80	79	159
Jim Dent	77	76	153	John Jacobs	75	84	159
Art Proctor	72	81	153	Charlie Sifford	79	80	159
Bob Diamond	77	77	154	Bob Moreland	80	80	160
Joe McDermott	75	79	154	Don Maddox	75	85	160
Bob Betley	77	77	154	Larry Wheeler	80	80	160
Pat O'Brien	75	79	154	Tom Joyce	78	82	160
Tony Perla	75	79	154	Mike McGinnis	77	83	160
Gene Borek	77	77	154	Jim Petralia	81	80	161
Carl Lohren	74	81	155	Jim Logue	79	82	161
Dave Eichelberger	80	75	155	George Shortridge	79	83	162
Chuck Montalbano	75	80	155	Ben Smith	79	83	162
Tom Wargo	77	78	155	Bob Hauer	82	81	163
El Collins	78	77	155	Lloyd Monroe	76	87	163
Gary Groh	75	80	155	Ed Sneed	77	87	164
Hiroshi Ishii	78	77	155	Terry Houser	80	84	164
Bruce Lehnhard	78	77	155	Bobby Stroble	83	82	165
Dave Barber	77	79	156	Arnold Palmer	84	82	166
Denny Lyons	81	75	156	John Brott	82	84	166
Tony Jacklin	74	82	156	Jimmy Wright	83	83	166
Homero Blancas	77	79	156	Lee Elder	80	87	167
George Glenn	78	79	157	Steve Oppermann	86	82	168
Bill Tindall	73	84	157	Doug Ford	84	85	169
Al Krueger	79	78	157	Ken Still	89	83	172
Masaru Amano	80	77	157	Freddie Haas	93	91	184
Simon Hobday	81	77	158	Bryan Abbott	72		WD
Harold Henning	82	76	158	Dick Hendrickson	79		WD
David Philo	80	78	158	Billy Maxwell	85		DQ
Steve Heckel	78	80	158				

Professionals completing 36 holes but not returning 72-hole scores received $775 each.

AT LONG LAST LOVE WINS HIS FIRST MAJOR

By Ron Sirak

If there was a time when it could have all gone wrong for Davis Love III at the 79th PGA Championship it was on the 16th hole of the final round. Stuck in that far corner of Winged Foot Golf Club, Love was faced not only with three enormously difficult closing holes, but he was also faced with his own past. Love was lugging the excess baggage of being known as one of the best golfers in the world never to have won a major championship.

British Open champion Justin Leonard, paired with Love, had just rolled in a 10-foot birdie putt on No. 15 to cut a lead that had been as large as five strokes to three strokes with three holes to play. As Leonard plucked his ball from the cup and strode to the 16th tee, his always grim expression was fiercer than usual. The eyes that flashed beneath the hat pulled low on his forehead seemed to say, "This is not over yet."

Making matters worse for Love was a sudden turn in the weather on that very same hole that dropped a curtain of clouds over Mamaroneck, New York, and unleashed a torrent of rain that was a cruel reminder of the tears shed by Love

Caddie and brother Mark Love provided encouragement.

Davis Love III tried unsuccessfully to get Justin Leonard to join him in the victory walk and ovations.

when he lost the 1996 U.S. Open by one stroke after he used three putts on the final hole.

Suddenly now, washing over Love and over all of those watching were memories of squandered opportunities in the 1995 Masters and of the series of missed putts on the back nine at Shinnecock Hills in the U.S. Open that same year that cost Love a chance at the title.

Most of all, the raindrops that dripped from Love's visor when he stepped up to drive off the 16th tee — a fairway he hadn't hit all week — fell like the tears he shed in 1988 when his father, Davis Jr., was killed in a plane crash.

It was the father, a respected PGA teaching professional, who first put a club in the child's hand and gave him the love of the game. It was the father to whom the child turned for support when things went wrong on the course. And when, at the age of just 24, Davis III lost Davis Jr., he was deprived of more than a father.

"I lost my teacher and my best friend on the same day," Love said. "He was the one I could call and tell about my bad shots. No one else wanted to hear about them."

Love won once on the PGA Tour before his father died, a victory at Hilton Head at the age of 23 that seemed to be the heralding of a great career. He went two years without winning following his father's death, then won seven times in the next four years.

But never in that stretch did he make a run at a major championship. He played in 28 majors until he finally got a top-10 finish, coming in second at the 1995 Masters when he could have won except that he was once again let down by his putter on the closing holes.

Each heartbreak endured by this extremely likeable young man was a sorrow shared with a loyal legion of fans, friends and fellow professionals who understood that Love was trying to win more than just a golf tournament, more than merely a major championship. It was as if the child was trying too hard to prove something to the missing father, to pay back the man who had given him so much by winning a major title in his memory. And everyone knew it. Everyone knew the story. Somehow, that made it all the more difficult.

Love, who was born the day after his father played in the 1964 Masters and who decided he wanted to be a professional golfer after watching his father play in this same PGA Championship in 1974, was faced with the most important tee shot of his life on No. 16.

"I hit three of the worst drives I could ever hit on that hole in the first three days," Love said afterward. "My brother (caddie Mark) told me, when we were talking about what club to hit off that tee this morning, he said the odds are very good you're going to hit the fairway today because you haven't been close yet."

Love had played the 16th hole two over par in the first three rounds while Leonard was making pars each day. "He said, 'Just hit a three wood and put a good swing on it,'" Love said about the advice from his brother. "And I hit a very good shot around the corner."

Love followed the gutsy tee shot with another great shot, a six iron to about 10 feet, and made the two-putt par. Leonard, who drove into the thick rough that was now soaked with rain and was like hitting out of seaweed, missed the green with his approach shot and made a bogey. Love was four strokes ahead with two holes to play and the tournament was over.

"Those two shots he hit at 16 in a downpour were just incredible," Leonard said, shaking his head with genuine awe.

As incredible as those shots were, their memory was almost swallowed up in the magical way the 79th PGA Championship ended. The 17th hole was also played in a driving rain and a steady shower still fell as Love and Leonard walked off the 18th tee, the outcome now clearly settled.

Golden sunlight and a rainbow provided a fitting backdrop to the conclusion of the 79th PGA Championship.

With each step Love took toward the final green, the sun fought to get from behind the clouds as if pushed by an unseen hand.

Then, almost as if to say that the dark days filled with all those missed opportunities and washed by all those tears were behind him, golden sunlight bathed the green and a brilliant rainbow arched over the majestic clubhouse.

Love's father used to have a simple bit of advice for his son: "Follow your dream and enjoy the trip." That trip was not always smooth but on this Sunday in August it became a dream come true.

"The son of a PGA member," Love said, choking back tears as he looked at the silver Wanamaker Trophy. "Who would have thought?"

Winged Foot has been the site of precious few major professional championships. It hosted the U.S. Open in 1929, 1959, 1974 and 1984. Although the very first PGA Championship was played at nearby Siwanoy Country Club in 1916, the title had never been contested at Winged Foot.

The great course had, however, produced great moments. In the 1929 U.S. Open, Bobby Jones made a 12-foot, downhill, double-breaking putt on the final hole to force a playoff with Al Espinosa. Jones won the next day. Many golf writers, including O.B. Keeler and Grantland Rice, felt that victory was the springboard to Jones' sweep of the U.S. Open, British Open, U.S. Amateur and British Amateur in 1930.

In 1984 Winged Foot witnessed the beginning of one of the most compelling stories of the next decade and a half. Greg Norman lost the U.S. Open in a playoff with Fuzzy Zoeller. It was the first of eight second-place finishes in majors by Norman and was the first leg of a dubious honor for Norman — The Near Slam.

He is the only player in history to lose all four

Love went five under par in four holes, the third through the sixth, for 66 in the opening round to share the lead.

The feature group had the three young major champions of 1997 — Tiger Woods, Ernie Els and Justin Leonard.

of the major championships in playoffs, although Craig Wood also came close. He lost the Masters, U.S. Open and British Open in playoffs and lost the PGA Championship in the final when it was match play.

The return of a major championship to Winged Foot seemed to demand that something special would happen. Perhaps Norman would return to the scene of his initial heartbreak and gain a measure of revenge. Perhaps veteran Tom Watson would win his first PGA Championship and complete the career Grand Slam. Perhaps Colin Montgomerie would get his first major ever after losing both a PGA Championship and a U.S. Open in playoffs and finishing second in another U.S. Open just two months earlier.

But the compelling confrontation that seemed to be brewing at Winged Foot was one of the generations. The 1997 golf season seemed to represent a changing of the guard in golf. Love was sort of an afterthought going into the PGA Championship. Although he was only 33, he seemed a bit of an old man compared to the winners of the three major championships already played.

Tiger Woods, 21, left the golf world — and the world at large — speechless when he not only won the first major championship he played in as a professional, but overwhelmed the field at the Masters in April by 12 strokes, the largest margin of victory in a major championship since the 1862 British Open.

Ernie Els won his second U.S. Open title at just 27 years of age when he outlasted Montgomerie, Tom Lehman and Jeff Maggert in a stirring final round at Congressional Country Club near Washington in June.

And the 25-year-old Leonard shot a 65 on Sunday — the only one of the 16 players who started the last round under par to break 70 that day — and won the British Open in July by outlasting

Jesper Parnevik and Darren Clarke, two other young players who appeared destined for great things.

"It's time for a changing of the guard," Woods said the week before the PGA Championship. "Guys like Tom Kite and Tom Watson were great players, but they are on their way out."

A new breed of golfers raised in the environment of a much more competitive college scene and nurtured on the Nike Tour were ready to win at a much earlier age. "People don't realize how good the Nike Tour has been for golf," Stewart Cink, 24, said about the eight-year-old minor league circuit on which he was the leading money winner in 1996. "It seems like we're seeing the results of it," Cink said. "We're more ready to win than probably any other era in golf."

In the 40 major championships played in the 10 years immediately previous to 1997, the average age of the winner was 33.1. The average age of the three winners in 1997 going into the PGA Championship was 24.3. "There's definitely an influx of good, young players," Woods said. "It's good for the game."

It was clearly The Year of the Kids and the talk going into Winged Foot was how this could be the first year since the Masters was first played in 1934 that all four of the major championships would be won by players under 30 years old.

The names tossed about on the practice tee, in the locker room and among the media as top contenders were — in addition to Woods, Els and Leonard — under-30 guys like Phil Mickelson, Jim Furyk, David Duval, Paul Stankowski and Cink.

"I'm not sure what the reason is," Leonard said about the changing of the guard. "I think in my case, I see guys like Tiger and Ernie, and seeing Phil Mickelson win his 11th tournament last week. Seeing that maybe raises my expectations a little bit."

While youthful players dominated the pre-tournament talk, three veteran players commanded some attention for different reasons of intrigue: Norman, Nick Faldo and John Daly.

Norman and Faldo, both now past 40, both missed the cut in the Masters, and when Norman missed the cut in the U.S. Open and was 36th in the British Open and Faldo finished 48th in the U.S. Open and 51st in the British Open, it was the first time in 15 years that one of those two hadn't contended in at least one of the majors.

If new faces were pushing their way onto the golfing map, Norman and Faldo were two longtime landmarks being edged aside. Winged Foot would be their last chance in 1997 to prove they were still factors in the majors.

Daly was another case entirely. The one-time Wiz Kid who had won both the PGA Championship and the British Open before his 30th birthday, was once again trying to bounce back after alcohol rehabilitation.

Daly's first major championship back following rehab was the U.S. Open at Congressional but, fearing he was on the verge of a re-occurrence of the tremors that are a frequent symptom of alcoholism and that bothered him the week before in the Kemper Open, Daly walked off the course after nine holes of the second round without telling his playing companions, tournament officials or even his caddie.

His return at the PGA Championship — the scene of his breakthrough victory at Crooked Stick in 1991 when he got in as the ninth alternate only when Nick Price dropped out because his wife was having a baby — was an attempt to prove he had returned to more than just golf. It was an attempt to prove he had his life under control, maybe for the first time.

Daly's presence at the PGA Championship, a tournament he won when he was only 25, seemed an almost morbid reminder of the youth theme going into Winged Foot. No one more than Daly, whose power and enthusiasm made him one of

A slimmer, sober John Daly started in championship form, posting 66 while showing control and patience.

the most popular players in the game, demonstrated the transient nature of youth and the mistakes it is bound to bring.

And swinging into Winged Foot, no one among the youthful challengers at the PGA Championship attracted more attention than Tiger Woods. He had already won four times on the PGA Tour in 1997 and had won an astounding six times in less than a year since turning professional. No one of the PGA Tour had won more than twice during that time period.

Woods' skill, enthusiasm, youth and ethnic background made him one of the most talked about and most watched figures in all of sports. As was the case everywhere Woods played in 1997, the galleries at Winged Foot were not only packed to capacity but were also a boisterous gathering representative of the new fans Woods was attracting to golf, most noticeably young people.

The enthusiastic New York crowds embraced Woods as one of their own.

There was also another engaging factor involving Woods coming into the PGA Championship. His coach, Butch Harmon, grew up on Winged Foot where his father, Claude, was the golf professional for 34 years. "It feels good to be here," Harmon said Monday as he walked a practice round with Woods. "It's like going home."

Harmon's knowledge of Winged Foot, a course of enormous subtlety where ball position is extremely important, seemed like a big edge for Woods. As Harmon walked with Woods in that Monday practice round he talked non-stop, parcelling out a vast warehouse of knowledge about the course. On each hole, Harmon had Woods toss balls into the massive greenside bunkers that are a signature of the course.

"Better watch that take-away," Harmon said

Bob Tway shot 68 in a hot group with Daly and Azinger.

Robert Allenby credited his 67 to his long, straight drives.

while observing as Woods hit from the bunker at No. 3. "Keep it steep," he said, referring to the swing arc needed to achieve the loft to clear the high lips of the bunkers. "And notice how the sand is not so deep," Harmon said. "It'll pop right out of there."

As Woods' caddie, Mike "Fluff" Cowan, eyed the back of the second green for the likely Sunday pin position, Harmon yelled: "Fluff, six more up and one to the right." Cowan paced it off and held the flagstick over an imaginary hole as Woods practiced chipping to it from the rough. "Oh man, that one's a killer," Harmon said about the pin position.

Winged Foot overall was expected to be a killer. Fairways lined with tall trees and steeply contoured greens protected by deep bunkers made it a shotmaker's course. Accuracy was essential. Rough grown by the tournament committee to about a half-foot made precision even more important.

The measure of mercy given to the players was that an unusually wet year had left Winged Foot softer than normal. Tee shots that might have run through the doglegs and into the gnarled rough took two small bounces and stayed in the fairway. The soft greens were more receptive to iron shots and the double-breaks and slick slopes putted just a tad slower than normally expected in the heat of August. At least that was the case early in the week.

With Winged Foot as vulnerable as it ever would be, the players pounced in Thursday's first round. A total of 22 players broke par and the youth movement was well represented as six of those shooting below 70 — Robert Allenby, Shigeki Maruyama, Leonard, Stankowski, Furyk and Mickelson — were under 30 years old. Three other young guys — Woods, Els and Duval — were at even-par 70.

Love, who played four holes in five under par beginning at No. 3, shared the first-round lead

Paul Azinger said the greens "putted beautifully."

Justin Leonard, with 68, needed just 24 putts.

with a four-under-par 66, but it was the man with whom he shared the lead who stole the show.

Daly, showing the kind of control and patience his game, and his life, had lacked until now, left the driver in the bag much of the day, walked along under an unfamiliar Hogan-style white hat and only casually acknowledged the large, rowdy gallery. "I used to pump my fist in the air when I made some putts and stuff," Daly said. "I don't know, I think I'm just more relaxed."

He was also 30 pounds slimmer after a nutrition and therapy program tied to his rehabilitation and he was painfully honest about the constant battle he fights with his demons. "I'm always scared what's going to happen next," Daly said. "Golf and this disease are pretty similar. Golf is an addiction and so is alcohol."

Driving with a three wood on the three closing holes — par-fours measuring 457, 449 and 448 yards — Daly hit drives of 301, 312 and 292 yards, all in the fairway, and was able to flip short irons right at the stick on the receptive greens, making putts of five feet, four feet and less than a foot to close with 31 for his 66 to tie the competitive course record set by Zoeller in the 1984 U.S. Open.

"It was three of the hardest holes in golf, or pretty close to them," Daly said. "It just really made my day. It's just a wonderful feeling to birdie all three of those."

Love also handled those holes, making birdies on Nos. 17 and 18 to get a share of the lead. "I holed a few putts right off the bat," Love said. "That gave me some confidence."

Allenby was in third place alone with 67 and eight players were tied at 68, including Maruyama, Leonard, Stankowski, Paul Azinger, Greg Norman and Tom Kite, who would captain the U.S. Ryder Cup Team in Spain the following month. "This is as easy as it is probably going to get," Kite said. "Winged Foot is not going to take this lying down."

Tiger Woods had a pair of 70s to start.

Woods was one of those who felt the kick of Winged Foot. For the third consecutive major championship he was plagued by a big-number hole that sabotaged otherwise fine play, making a double-bogey seven on No. 12 when he drove into the right rough and needed four shots to get out.

Woods played in the glamour group of the day, with Els and Leonard, as the winners of the year's first three major championships were paired together. "It was neat because we were kind of trading off birdies," Woods said. "You're feeding off one another and you can definitely feel the positive energy out there. We are going to be playing against each other for about 20 years and that is going to be really neat."

Woods and Els outplayed Leonard, but Leonard outscored them. The British Open champion hit only seven greens in regulation but, beginning with an intentionally bladed sand wedge that found the hole on No. 9, needed only 11 putts over the last 10 holes and shot 68, two better than Woods and Els and two behind Daly and Love.

"I made all the putts I needed to make inside eight or 10 feet," Leonard said after using only 24 putts compared to 32 by Woods. "You know, I can't last like that all week."

Kite was correct in predicting that Winged Foot would not take the birdie barrage lying down. The A.W. Tillinghast course grew some teeth for Friday's second round.

Leonard was wrong, at least for the time being. He was able to "last like that" at least for one more day. This time he hit six greenside bunkers and five times was able to scramble to save pars as he shot 70. This time he used only 25 putts.

"To keep myself in the tournament with my short game, I do feel good about that," Leonard said after blasting from a bunker on the final hole and making a 12-foot par-saving putt to be tied at 138 with Mickelson, Maggert, Maruyama, Costantino Rocca, Fred Couples and Phil Blackmar, two strokes behind 36-hole leader Lee Janzen. Love was sandwiched in between at 137.

After Winged Foot was a generous host on Thursday, suddenly it was as if the air was sucked off the course on Friday as the fairways seemed tighter, the rough seemed higher, the bunkers bigger and the greens faster.

In a perfect example of the way the pressure increases with each round of a major championship, the leaders came back to the field in the second round and the guys who kept the ball in play and had touch around the greens crept up the leaderboard.

Only four of the 22 players who broke par in the first round could match that feat on Friday. Four under par was leading after 18 holes and it was still leading after 36 holes.

At the end of a round that had the desperate feel of watching a person swim for survival in a choppy sea, Janzen — who played 18 holes in 62 strokes beginning with No. 10 on Thursday —

Despite two closing bogeys, Lee Janzen led with 67-136.

had the lead and was making a strong bid to get onto the U.S. Ryder Cup Team.

Even Janzen and Love took their lumps from Winged Foot on Friday. Janzen finished with bogeys on the last two holes and Love made a double bogey on No. 16 on his way to 71. "I've made plenty of mistakes and I'm still on top of the leaderboard," Janzen said. "It's a game of momentum."

Such tournament-tough players as Woods, Norman, Furyk, Lehman, Daly, Kite and Payne Stewart were within five strokes of the lead after 36 holes.

"It is playing brutally tough," Daly said after shooting 73 to be at one-under-par 139, three strokes off the lead. "The greens were firming up and the pins were in some tough places," he said. "I didn't play that bad. You just can't get the ball near the hole out there."

Woods made a move early in the round when he started with two consecutive birdies but made too many wild shots into the sand and high grass

Love slipped to second at 137 with poor putting.

Costantino Rocca, at 138, was happy to be under par.

Phil Mickelson completed 36 holes with a pair of 69s.

Fred Couples holed out for an eagle at No. 11.

and finished with his second consecutive 70. "I didn't really mis-hit a shot," Woods said. "I misplaced some."

The third member of the glamour group — Els — stumbled to 76 and was nine strokes back at 146.

Faldo shot 78 and missed the cut along with defending PGA Champion Mark Brooks, who became the first person to win a major championship and then miss the cut in all four majors the next year.

The compelling subtext that adds to the intrigue of the PGA Championship every two years — the race to make the U.S. Ryder Cup Team in what is the final qualifying tournament — took several fascinating twists in the first two rounds.

Tommy Tolles, who was trying to hang onto his spot on the team and desperately needed a top-10 finish, was seven strokes back at 143 after 36 holes. To make matters worse, Maggert, who was trying to break into the top 10, was looking good at 138.

Phil Blackmar improved two strokes to 68 in the second round despite only four fairways hit but 11 one-putt greens.

Janzen and Couples were making strong cases to be selected as Captain's picks for the U.S. Team and Kite saw his wildcard selection process become more difficult with the strong performance of a seven-time Ryder Cup veteran — himself.

Coming into the PGA Championship, Kite was concerned that no one outside the top 10 was playing well enough to be included on the team. "What I need is someone stepping forward this week and making a statement," Kite said. "I have a lot of guys wanting to be on the team. But they aren't making a statement."

In fact, four of the top 10 U.S. players at the end of January had played their way out of the top 10. And of those four — Steve Jones, Kenny Perry, Brooks and Couples — only Couples had played well enough recently to even merit consideration for a Captain's choice. And what about Kite himself? "I would have to do something spectacular to impress the Captain, that's for sure," Kite said.

Shigeki Maruyama played his first PGA Championship.

At 138, Jeff Maggert said he liked Championship courses.

Defending Champion Mark Brooks missed the cut.

Vijay Singh posted 66–139 in the second round.

Kite was doing just that through the first two rounds of the PGA Championship, following his 68 with 71 to be at 139, just three strokes back going into the weekend. Even a victory wouldn't get Kite into the top 10 and gain an automatic spot. But with his second-place finish at the Masters and his great record in Ryder Cup play, it would make it difficult to pass himself up as a Captain's pick. Even Captain Kite would have to admit that Player Kite deserved to be on the team.

Meanwhile, things were pretty grim for the European Ryder Cup Team members. Of the 12 men who would end up on the European Team, four — Ian Woosnam, Jose Maria Olazabal, Darren Clarke and Faldo — missed the cut at Winged Foot.

After 36 holes at the PGA Championship, the 12 guys who would become the European Ryder Cup Team were a collective 67 over par. The 12 players who represented the U.S. at Valderrama were a collective eight over par, a smashing 59-stroke victory by the Americans.

Love's 66 gained him a share of the lead at 203.

If Saturday is moving day in every tournament, it was the day Love and Leonard cleaned house at the PGA Championship. It was also the day Daly came undone.

It was almost as if the strain of the first two rounds had worn down Daly both physically and mentally. After driving so well with his three wood in the first two rounds, he inexplicably went back to his driver in the third round. After missing fairway after fairway, he finally lost all composure and tossed that driver over a fence on the 12th hole after yet another bad tee shot on his way to 77.

As the also-rans teed off early in the day on Saturday, the heat crept up silently on the course. While such celebrities as heavyweight champion Evander Holyfield, still showing a pink scar from the bite Mike Tyson took out of his ear, and Miss Universe jockeyed to catch a glimpse of Woods, Love and Leonard were sneaking away from the field.

The greens at Winged Foot had the yellow sheen of aged wax on a linoleum floor, putted just

Leonard set the course record with 65 in the third round.

The question was whether Tom Kite, the golfer, was making a good enough impression on Tom Kite, the Captain.

Janzen's 74 and 210 total dropped him seven strokes behind, but Janzen said, "By no means am I out of it."

as fast and in Saturday's third round sent all but Love and Leonard slipping away.

On a day when the temperature climbed into the 90s and the humidity made it feel like 103 degrees, 15 players started the round under par but only Love and Leonard were in red numbers when the day ended. That broke the PGA Championship record-low of three players under par after 54 holes set in 1975 at Firestone Country Club in Akron, Ohio.

Leonard with 65 and Love with 66 shot the two lowest scores of a day marred by a two-hour rain and lightning delay and finished 54 holes tied at seven-under-par 203, seven strokes ahead of Kite and Janzen and virtually eliminating everyone but themselves. "This afternoon it was a completely different golf course than we played the last couple of days," Love said. "The greens were a lot faster and a lot harder and a lot more difficult."

Leonard, trying to become the first player to win consecutive major championships since Nick Price won the British Open and the PGA Championship back-to-back in 1994, played with enormous control in the third round, unlike his scrambling play of the first two days when he was saved by his wedge and his putter. This time, Leonard hit 15 of 18 greens in regulation. His 65 broke the course record by one stroke.

A ticklish, eight-foot, downhill birdie putt on the final hole gave Leonard the course record and put him in the clubhouse at seven-under-par 203. "I think my experience from the British Open enabled me to play well today," Leonard said. "Having been in that situation just four weeks ago, I think I'll be able to draw on that experience and that should help me tomorrow."

Love, playing three holes behind Leonard, made two 10-foot par-saving putts on Nos. 16 and 17 after the rain delay and then made virtually the same putt as Leonard on the final hole for 66. Only six players beside Love and Leonard shot in the 60s on Saturday and only one of those, Scott Hoch, was within seven strokes of the lead coming into the third round. And Hoch lost ground with his 68.

Scott Hoch's 68 gave him a 211 total.

Kite was at even-par 210 after another 71, along with Janzen. Woods, Couples, Mickelson, Duval, Hoch and Maggert were at 211, eight strokes back. Of those, only Woods carried with him the real threat of being able to push the course record another stroke lower to 64 and getting back into the picture on Sunday. Woods' astounding 63-64 finish the last two rounds at Pebble Beach in February proved he was never really out of a tournament.

But it did appear that Sunday was going to be a showdown between Love and Leonard. "I'm going to have that trying-to-win-the-first-one pressure," Love said. "But it all comes down to who can hit the best shots. I don't think I've ever been as comfortable in a big tournament with the way I'm playing."

Norman, who was in the hunt until he made a double bogey on No. 16 and a bogey on the 17th hole on Saturday to fall to three over par, said, "The greens are two feet faster today than they were yesterday."

Woods floated in and out of the picture during the third round as he was once again plagued by even more big-number holes. He made a double bogey on the fourth hole, when he drove into the right rough, chunked it back to the fairway and then hit the right bunker.

He made an eagle on the 12th hole but made a bogey on No. 13 when he drove into the right rough. Woods made a sensational birdie on No. 16 when he hit a cut six iron from 171 yards under tree limbs, around some more trees and within nine feet of the hole. But he finished with a double bogey and a bogey on the last two holes and walked off the final green as if he had injured himself.

"The only thing I hurt was my ego," Woods said.

If Woods had been able to eliminate big-number holes he would have contended in every major championship in 1997. He had three double bogeys in the U.S. Open, two triple bogeys and a quadruple bogey in the British Open and would finish with four double bogeys in the PGA Championship. Thoughts of that nature were clearly on his mind as he stomped off the 18th green on Saturday. "There's nothing wrong," Woods said. "I'm just angry."

While Woods has shown the ability to use his anger in a positive way on the golf course, Daly let his anger, and his desire to please the crowd, get the best of him in the third round. After driving perfectly on the first two holes, using his three wood and plopping 290-yard shots onto the fairway, he started using his driver and started exploring the farthest reaches of Winged Foot.

He missed the fourth and fifth fairways and

After his 71, David Duval was one of six at 211.

A spectacular six-iron shot at the 16th was off-set by Woods' two closing bogeys as he finished at 71–211.

Two disasters — a double bogey here at the fifth and a triple bogey at the 16th — left Mickelson at 73–211.

then tried to drive the 324-yard sixth hole. Instead, he drove into the right rough, dumped his second shot into the bunker, blasted 20 feet above the hole and three-putted for a double bogey. After missing the eighth and the 11th fairways, Daly lost control of another drive on No. 12 and then sent his driver into the woods and over a fence where it was retrieved by a spectator and returned to Daly. He later described the heave as "a toss."

"Basically, it's one day at a time and one shot at a time," Daly said about his struggle for control on and off the golf course. "I believe I've had 15 chances in life," he said when asked if this was a second chance for him. "I've had a lot of chances in life. That's all I can say about it."

Daly got into a verbal scuffle with a rules official in the final round when he again tried to drive the sixth green. It seemed like he would do the wise thing and hit a four iron, as most players were doing on the short par-four.

As the crowd yelled, "Go for it, John," and "We'll wait for the green to clear," Daly — with "Grip It and Rip It" stitched on the back of his pants — pulled the driver from his bag and unleashed his long, strong swing. This time he hooked it wildly left behind the rain shelter near the seventh tee. Daly, who became upset when he was denied a free drop, apparently misunderstood the rule. A player may receive swing and stance relief from an immovable object, but not line-of-sight relief. While Daly could strike the ball without obstruction, he did not have a clear line to the flag.

Still, Daly shot a solid 70 and finished 29th, an impressive return to major championship golf and a performance filled with both positive and negative signs about his progress toward controlling his inner demons.

All players have demons of different kinds they must contain in order to be champions. Ben Hogan had his hook. A young Nick Faldo needed to find a swing that would hold up under pres-

Couples shot a third-round 73 and fell from two to eight strokes behind.

sure. Greg Norman still fights the menacing monster that has deprived him of a major championship on American soil.

Davis Love III went into the final round of the 79th PGA Championship facing not only Justin Leonard, but also fighting his past. Would it be his legacy to be remembered as one of the greatest golfers never to win a major championship?

On Monday of PGA Championship week, one of the holders of that title, "Lighthorse" Harry Cooper was honored at an awards dinner near Winged Foot. Now 92 but still giving lessons five days a week at Westchester Country Club, Cooper — whose nickname came from his fast play — won 31 times on the PGA Tour, 13th on the all-time list. Everyone above Copper on the list has won major championships. Cooper, who was second in the Masters twice and second in the U.S. Open two more times, never won a major.

"They say I'm the best golfer never to win a major," Cooper said as he received his award.

"Well, all those other guys are dead and I'm still alive, so I think I did pretty well," he said to thunderous laughter.

Maybe Love will feel that way when he is 92 but now, at 33, he wanted this title. He wanted to put to rest once and for all any doubts that he was one of the premier golfers of his generation. And then there was the matter of fulfilling what he saw as a responsibility to his father, rewarding the man who first put a club in his hand.

When Ben Crenshaw won the 1995 Masters just days after serving as pallbearer for his lifelong teacher, Harvey Penick, he was carried along for the last few holes by a wildly supportive and emotional gallery. Crenshaw said he felt those cheers were not for him but for unseen people not on the course that day. "Everyone has someone who first put a club in their hand," Crenshaw explained. "When they saw me winning for Harvey, they all thought of the person who first put a club in their hand."

The brothers Love took aim at the major title that had been Davis' goal since watching their father in 1974.

In that way, perhaps Love, who let the U.S. Open slip away a year earlier on Father's Day, was playing that final Sunday at the PGA Championship not just for himself and his father but for the father, or coach, who first placed a club in the hand of everyone watching.

When Love and Leonard stepped to the first tee in the final group on a sweltering Sunday, their shirts were already damp with perspiration. It was also clear by the time they teed off that all other competition had melted away in the stifling heat. The championship would be decided in this final group, between Love and Leonard. No one else was making a serious run.

The Ryder Cup subplot, meanwhile, was being decided all over the course.

Maggert earned his way onto the team with a final-round 65 that tied Leonard's course record. He finished third at Winged Foot and knocked Tolles off the team. Tolles put up a brilliant rush to try to hold onto to his spot, shooting a 66 on Sunday, but it only got him to 13th in the PGA Championship and did not get any of the points he needed to make it to Spain.

Janzen closed with a strong 69 and finished fourth and would be rewarded the next morning when Kite announced that Janzen was one of his two Captain's picks. The other Captain's choice was Couples, who finished 29th at Winged Foot, but a 67 in the third round proved he was still capable, and his experience in four Ryder Cups was much needed on the young team.

The European Ryder Cup members, meanwhile, did not distinguish themselves at Winged Foot. Montgomerie finished 13th at the PGA Championship, but only Bernhard Langer and Lee Westwood joined him in the top 30.

Love and Leonard started the day tied for the lead, but the situation changed with shocking suddenness. Leonard made a bogey on No. 2 when he drove into the right rough and could only pitch back to the fairway. Love made a birdie putt from 23 feet on the third hole, and the lead grew to three strokes on the next hole when Leonard made a bogey after driving into the left rough.

The essential message sent by Winged Foot all week remained the same on Sunday: To have a chance of mastering this course you must put the tee shot in the fairway. In just four holes, Love had gone from tied with Leonard to three strokes ahead.

"He got off to a good start but I didn't and I think that was the key to the day," Leonard said.

Maggert placed third to earn a Ryder Cup berth.

Leonard struggled with 37 on the first nine of the final round, finishing second but five strokes behind at 71–274.

Janzen finished with 69 and, with a 279 total, held fourth place alone.

Blackmar took a share of sixth place, closing with 69 for his 281 total.

"Those first few holes were difficult and then you've got a couple of birdie holes at five and six," he said. "I was just trying to get into a good rhythm, which I didn't in the first few holes."

While Leonard struggled off the tee, Love played with calm precision, shooting 32 on the front nine to Leonard's 37. The lead was five strokes at the turn and Leonard never got closer than three strokes coming in.

While the drive and the second shot in the rain at No. 16 put the tournament away for Love, it was a less well-played hole that gave him the confidence that he could hold on.

Leonard made a birdie on No. 12 and Love, whose drive was "pulled into the really deep rough," made a bogey. The two-stroke swing pulled Leonard within three strokes of the lead. "Justin made his for birdie and I missed (from six feet for par) and I thought that turned it back for him to have a really big chance," Love said.

After the tee shots on No. 13, that seemed like it would be a self-fulfilling prophecy. "Thirteen was the hole that really saved me," Love said about the 212-yard par-three. Leonard, hitting

Kite had an even-par 280 total.

Tommy Tolles played well, having a 66–284 finish.

Jim Furyk shot 68 to share sixth place.

first, knocked a three iron to 15 feet right behind the flag, a very makeable birdie putt. Love, meanwhile, hit a four iron into the high grass left of the green. "Honestly, the only really, really bad shots I hit were on that hole," Love said. "I hit a bad four iron yesterday (when he made a bogey) and a bad four iron today."

But on Sunday, he made up for the bad shot with a great one. "I got a semi-decent lie in the matted rough and I flipped an L-wedge and it almost went in the hole," Love said. "I think that saved the tournament for me. That gave me the confidence that I could get up-and-down from anywhere, I could handle anything."

Leonard missed his birdie putt and what could have been the second two-stroke swing in two holes, cutting the lead to one stroke, ended up being a halved hole.

Love got the lead back to four strokes when Leonard missed another fairway on No. 14 and made a bogey. Leonard's birdie on No. 15 cut the lead to three strokes, but that was when Love reached inside himself and found what he needed to close like a true champion.

"I'm disappointed," Leonard said. "I felt good coming into today. He just played very well."

Love played very well indeed. He closed with yet another 66, his third of the week. Only two scores the entire tournament — the 65 by Leonard on Saturday and the 65 by Maggert on Sunday — were lower than the 66 Love shot in three of the four rounds.

Love's 11-under-par 269 overwhelmed Leonard by five strokes and he was seven ahead of Maggert and 10 better than Janzen, who finished fourth. Love's 269 would have won the 1984 U.S. Open at Winged Foot by seven strokes, and his victory in the PGA Championship meant that the last 13 majors were won by 13 different people.

Kite closed with a 70 and was the only player at even-par 280, fifth best in the field. He would reveal the next day that he had decided months earlier that he would not pick himself to the Ryder Cup Team if he did not play his way onto it. "But

Even-par 70 in the last round brought Tom Lehman among the top 10 finishers.

I couldn't tell you guys that, could I?" Kite said to a room full of reporters. Certainly, if anyone else was Captain of the U.S. Ryder Cup Team, Tom Kite would have been one of the two captain's picks. He deserved it.

Love's victory, which was not only a victory but an overwhelming performance, went a long way toward making up for past disappointments and toward lifting him to the next level of players. "He's been under an awful lot of pressure for four or five years," Leonard said. "Having shed that title or whatever you want to call it, that takes an awful lot of pressure off of him. Now, the sky is the limit."

The burden of being known as the best player in the world without a major title now passes to Montgomerie and Mickelson.

A year ago on Father's Day, Love slumped in despair as he let the U.S. Open slip way on the final green. He never let matters get as far as the final green at Winged Foot. This time, he would not let down his father. "I think about him a lot," Love said. "I thought about him a lot today. I think he would have said it was my turn. I think he would have been very proud."

Playing most of the last four holes in the driving rain, Love washed away any chance Leonard had for a miracle comeback by playing the final six holes one under par.

"It was hard to get through those last three holes without breaking down," Love said, tears now filling his eyes. As he neared the 18th green, Love tried to get Leonard to share the walk, and the ovation, with him. "I've got a lot of great friends on this tour and I played with one of them today," Love said. "I wanted to beat him so bad, but I couldn't look at him … I didn't want it to be him."

As Love put his arm around Leonard and urged him to join in his victory walk, Leonard gently moved away. "You go," Leonard said. "It's yours."

After the final putt fell, Love swung his visor through the air and hugged Leonard. Then, with tears rolling down his cheeks, he fell into emo-

Love played the final six holes in one under par, a rousing finish that precluded a comeback by any challengers.

tional embraces first with his brother, Mark, then his wife, Robin, and his mother, Penta.

"It's been a long time," Love said as he lifted the silver Wanamaker Trophy into the air and gave it a kiss. "I'm looking forward to taking this and running with it and turning it into a lot more chances."

Love thought back to the day when he decided he wanted to be a professional golfer. It was at the 1974 PGA Championship at Tanglewood Golf Club near Winston-Salem, North Carolina, and Love's Charlotte birthplace. Lee Trevino won that tournament and Jack Nicklaus finished second. But Love has a different memory. "My father played in the tournament and I was mesmerized by the atmosphere," Love said. "I thought to myself, 'Man, this is the life.'"

Perhaps a few years down the road, Davis Love IV, not yet four years old when his father won the PGA Championship, will watch his father and decide to become the next generation of professional golfer in the Love family. If so, he likely will be motivated as much by his father's gentle nature as by his golfing skills.

"A lot of people have told me I don't have the killer instinct, I don't have the meanness to win," Love said. "I don't think you have to have that. I think you have to beat the golf course. I think you have to play the game. Justin Leonard was a true champion out there today finishing second."

Leonard reacted like a true champion. "I'm disappointed," Leonard said. "Obviously, going into the day I thought I had a good chance, but at the same time I'm happy for Davis and his family. I know this is something they've waited for a long time." Then, putting into words something everyone felt, Leonard summed up the day: "It's good for golf."

Love was where he dreamed of being.

What started out as the Summer of Youth in golf ended up as the Summer of Love.

No one ever was a more deserving champion than Love. If fate ever conspired to make good things happen to good people, it was that glorious week at Winged Foot when Love completed his long climb to the top — when he finally won his first major at the PGA Championship. "We threw a lot of them away," Love said about his squandered opportunities in major championships. "But we got this one."

Love left nothing to chance in that final round. He took the game right to Leonard and never let the pressure ease. Maybe he lacks a killer instinct, but he clearly possesses a love of the game, and sometimes that is enough.

This performance at the 79th PGA Championship was something a teaching professional like Davis Love Jr. would have appreciated.

His smile likely would have been as bright and as broad as the rainbow that arched over the sky late that Sunday afternoon and welcomed Davis Love III to the world of major championship winners.

79th PGA Championship

August 14-17, 1997, Winged Foot Golf Club, Mamaroneck, New York

Contestant	Rounds				Total	Prize
Davis Love III	66	71	66	66	269	$470,000.00
Justin Leonard	68	70	65	71	274	280,000.00
Jeff Maggert	69	69	73	65	276	175,000.00
Lee Janzen	69	67	74	69	279	125,000.00
Tom Kite	68	71	71	70	280	105,000.00
Phil Blackmar	70	68	74	69	281	85,000.00
Jim Furyk	69	72	72	68	281	85,000.00
Scott Hoch	71	72	68	70	281	85,000.00
Tom Byrum	69	73	70	70	282	70,000.00
Tom Lehman	69	72	72	70	283	60,000.00
Scott McCarron	74	71	67	71	283	60,000.00
Joey Sindelar	72	71	71	69	283	60,000.00
David Duval	70	70	71	73	284	35,100.00
Tim Herron	72	73	68	71	284	35,100.00
Colin Montgomerie	74	71	67	72	284	35,100.00
Greg Norman	68	71	74	71	284	35,100.00
Nick Price	72	70	72	70	284	35,100.00
Vijay Singh	73	66	76	69	284	35,100.00
Tommy Tolles	75	70	73	66	284	35,100.00
Kirk Triplett	73	70	71	70	284	35,100.00
Bob Tway	68	75	72	69	284	35,100.00
Mark O'Meara	69	73	75	67	284	35,100.00
Mark Calcavecchia	71	74	73	67	285	22,500.00
Bernhard Langer	73	71	72	69	285	22,500.00
Doug Martin	69	75	74	67	285	22,500.00
Shigeki Maruyama	68	70	74	73	285	22,500.00
Kenny Perry	73	68	73	71	285	22,500.00
John Cook	71	71	74	69	285	22,500.00
Paul Azinger	68	73	71	74	286	13,625.00
Ronnie Black	76	69	71	70	286	13,625.00
Fred Couples	71	67	73	75	286	13,625.00
John Daly	66	73	77	70	286	13,625.00
Paul Goydos	70	72	71	73	286	13,625.00
Hale Irwin	73	70	71	72	286	13,625.00
Phil Mickelson	69	69	73	75	286	13,625.00
Frank Nobilo	72	73	67	74	286	13,625.00
Don Pooley	72	74	70	70	286	13,625.00
Payne Stewart	70	70	72	74	286	13,625.00
Lee Westwood	74	68	71	73	286	13,625.00
Tiger Woods	70	70	71	75	286	13,625.00
Ignacio Garrido	70	71	75	71	287	8,375.00
Steve Jones	69	73	75	70	287	8,375.00
David Ogrin	74	72	71	70	287	8,375.00
Eduardo Romero	71	72	72	72	287	8,375.00
Thomas Bjorn	72	68	77	71	288	7,375.00
Steve Elkington	72	72	70	74	288	7,375.00
Jesper Parnevik	76	70	71	71	288	7,375.00
Sam Torrance	74	72	70	72	288	7,375.00
Robert Allenby	67	77	74	71	289	6,375.00
Brian Henninger	74	68	75	72	289	6,375.00
Chris Perry	68	71	73	77	289	6,375.00
Loren Roberts	76	70	74	69	289	6,375.00
Olin Browne	70	73	74	73	290	5,280.00
Ernie Els	70	76	74	70	290	5,280.00
Billy Mayfair	75	68	75	72	290	5,280.00

79TH PGA CHAMPIONSHIP

Contestant	Rounds				Total	Prize
Taylor Smith	71	71	74	74	290	5,280.00
Craig Stadler	72	72	74	72	290	5,280.00
Steve Lowery	72	69	79	71	291	4,700.00
Larry Mize	71	73	73	74	291	4,700.00
Lanny Wadkins	72	72	77	70	291	4,700.00
Stuart Appleby	75	70	69	78	292	4,333.34
Jay Haas	71	69	73	79	292	4,333.34
Russ Cochran	72	73	72	75	292	4,333.33
Fred Funk	71	74	77	70	292	4,333.33
Retief Goosen	72	70	74	76	292	4,333.33
Lee Rinker	70	71	75	76	292	4,333.33
Peter Jacobsen	74	72	75	72	293	4,100.00
Per-Ulrik Johansson	73	69	73	78	293	4,100.00
Paul Stankowski	68	71	77	77	293	4,100.00
Carlos Franco	69	74	76	75	294	4,000.00
Michael Bradley	73	69	80	73	295	3,875.00
Yoshinori Kaneko	72	73	76	74	295	3,875.00
Larry Nelson	76	70	76	73	295	3,875.00
Costantino Rocca	69	69	79	78	295	3,875.00
Andrew Magee	71	70	80	75	296	3,750.00
Pete Jordan	76	70	75	76	297	3,675.00
Kevin Sutherland	73	73	73	78	297	3,675.00

Out of Final 36 Holes

Contestant	R1	R2	Total	Contestant	R1	R2	Total
Billy Andrade	72	75	147	Clarence Rose	74	77	151
Bob Boyd	71	76	147	Jeff Sluman	74	77	151
Jim Carter	73	74	147	Bob Sowards	74	77	151
Rick Fehr	72	75	147	Michael Burke, Jr.	77	75	152
David Frost	76	71	147	Ed Fiori	76	76	152
Len Mattiace	72	75	147	Jose Maria Olazabal	79	73	152
Billy Ray Brown	76	72	148	Duffy Waldorf	74	78	152
Robert Damron	76	72	148	Darren Clarke	74	79	153
Glen Day	76	72	148	Frank Dobbs	80	73	153
Padraig Harrington	77	71	148	Nick Faldo	75	78	153
Jeffrey Lankford	72	76	148	Steve Schneiter	75	78	153
Craig Parry	74	74	148	Curtis Strange	76	77	153
Ron Philo, Jr.	72	76	148	Chris Tucker	78	75	153
Steve Stricker	73	75	148	Bruce Zabriski	76	77	153
David Toms	73	75	148	Peter Lonard	75	79	154
Fuzzy Zoeller	73	75	148	Bob Makoski	79	75	154
Guy Boros	81	68	149	Mike Standly	76	78	154
Mike Brisky	75	74	149	John Lee	74	81	155
Paul Broadhurst	74	75	149	Pete Oakley	78	77	155
Mark Brooks	70	79	149	Brian Watts	78	77	155
Bob Ford	74	75	149	Shawn Kelly	76	80	156
John Mazza	71	78	149	Hal Sutton	78	78	156
Jay Overton	77	72	149	Rob Wilkin	78	78	156
Chris Toulson	75	74	149	Ben Crenshaw	77	80	157
Ian Woosnam	77	72	149	Jerry Kelly	81	76	157
Robert Gamez	74	76	150	Jim White	82	75	157
Kelly Gibson	76	74	150	Wayne Grady	79	79	158
Dudley Hart	74	76	150	James Mason	78	80	158
Mike Hulbert	75	75	150	John Hickson	76	84	160
Jack Nicklaus	74	76	150	Darrell Kestner	79	83	162
Naomichi (Joe) Ozaki	75	75	150	Mark Fuller	79	84	163
John Stone	75	75	150	John Paesani	79	85	164
Tom Watson	71	79	150	Bret Taylor	82	83	165
Jay Don Blake	73	78	151	Mark Wiebe	77		WD
Brandel Chamblee	77	74	151	John Mahaffey	78		WD
Stewart Cink	76	75	151	Frankie Minoza	80		WD
Brad Faxon	73	78	151				

Professionals completing 36 holes but not returning 72-hole scores received $1,200 each.

EUROPE REIGNS IN SEVE'S SPAIN FOR RYDER CUP

By Leonard Shapiro

The 32nd Ryder Cup Matches ended much the same way they had begun, with a pelting rain dousing hundreds of hardy spectators. They had gathered around the Valderrama clubhouse for a wet and wild victory celebration for a European Team that toasted and soaked each other with popping champagne bottles, all the while singing "olé, olé, olé" in tribute to the man many said had willed them to victory.

The Ryder Cup now belongs to Europe for another two years. They had been a clear underdog going against an American Team many had said may have been the best group to have played in these Matches in almost 20 years. But Seve Ballesteros, the swashbuckling Spaniard who captained Europe in the first Ryder Cup ever contested on Spanish soil, clearly was the hero in Sotogrande, hard by the Rock of Gibraltar off the southern Mediterranean coast.

For the fifth time in the last seven tries, Europe had triumphed, by the typically narrowest of margins, a 14½-to-13½ decision despite a spirited American comeback, spurred by a pep talk from former President George Bush the night be-

Even the pelting rain could not stop the celebration after Europe

defeated the United States with a 14½-to-13½ decision in the 32nd Ryder Cup Matches at Valderrama.

fore, on the final day of singles when all had seemed lost after the first two days of team competition.

With the rat-a-tat-tat of raindrops splashing on umbrellas providing the background beat as the Ryder Cup was passed from one European Team member to another as they stood on the clubhouse steps, Ballesteros insisted only the rain was dripping down his face, and not a single tear.

"I was prepared for this moment," he would say later. "It is all in the mind. If you are mentally prepared and you control yourself, you do not cry."

Ballesteros had played on the winning 1995 European Team, just as he had played in all but one Ryder Cup since 1979. Almost always, he was a dominating, fiery force, with a 20-12-5 record. He cheered passionately from the sidelines for his teammates, exhorting them with pumping fists and bearish hugs.

That is also how he approached his 1997 captaincy in an event being played in his home country for the first time as a tribute to Ballesteros at a Valderrama golf course he also had a small hand in tweaking.

The 17th hole, a 511-yard par-five with a natural amphitheater around its water-fronted green and plenty of potential for high drama, was his creation. It became the most controversial — and in the end pivotal — patch of land on the property, criticized by players on both sides. They didn't like a 20-yard stretch of rough that split the fairway 290 yards down from the tee and took the driver out of the hands of the long hitters.

Europe's Colin Montgomerie had been sharply critical of the hole himself, saying, "It's the worst hole we play all year ... It's just hideous." Ballesteros clearly disagreed. "What is different about having rough in the middle of a fairway or a bunker?" he said. "If that rough is not there, players would hit driver and seven iron. This is a par-five, not a par-four ... Players who don't like 17 don't know how to manage the hole ... I'm proud of that hole. If they are not comfortable, all they have to do is win 3 and 2."

Former President George Bush spoke to the team then watched with his wife Barbara.

By contrast, American Captain Tom Kite had not been quite as vocal. He approached his position just as he has always approached his own game, with a work ethic and a will to win second to none. The consummate grinder, always the first man to arrive at the practice grounds and the last to leave, Kite seemingly left no detail to chance.

By all measures — world rankings, tournaments and major championships won — the Americans should have been favored. Nine U.S. players were in the top 16 of the world rankings, including No. 2 Tiger Woods. The Europeans had only one player in the top 10 — Montgomerie — and eight of their 12 men were not even in the top 25, with the lowest Denmark's Thomas Bjorn at No. 73.

Three of the four major championship winners — Woods (Masters), Justin Leonard (British Open) and Davis Love III (PGA Championship) — were on the U.S. side. The Europeans still had virtually the same solid core of veterans who had helped carry the team over the last 10 years, save for Ballesteros, whose balky back had made him

Jesper Parnevik (left) and Per-Ulrik Johansson started with a fourball victory over Tom Lehman and Jim Furyk.

Fred Couples (left) congratulated Brad Faxon on his winning putt in the opening fourballs.

Costantino Rocca (standing) and Jose Maria Olazabal scored Europe's first point in a narrow victory.

Captain Tom Kite (center) saw Mark O'Meara and Tiger Woods win in the morning and lose in the afternoon.

a shell of the creative, instinctive player he once was.

England's Nick Faldo, playing in his record 11th competition, had 21 Ryder Cup victories, the most ever by a European player, going into Valderrama. Ian Woosnam of Wales and Scotland's Montgomerie, Spain's Jose Maria Olazabal and Germany's Bernhard Langer all were multiple Ryder Cup participants. Experience under the enormous pressure, especially in playing a tricky course that was a frequent venue on the PGA European Tour, clearly became a factor once play began.

There were four American first-timers — Woods, Leonard, Jim Furyk and Scott Hoch — and five European rookies — Bjorn of Denmark, Jesper Parnevik of Sweden, Darren Clarke of Northern Ireland, Lee Westwood of England and Ignacio Garrido of Spain.

For a change, there was little controversy over Kite's two Captain's selections — Fred Couples and Lee Janzen. Kite actually was second-guessed on only one thing: Why, he was asked, didn't he pick himself? After all, he had finished second in the Masters and had three top-10 finishes in the majors in 1997. But Kite believed he couldn't be an effective leader if he was also playing and, as usual, made the sensible decision to stay out of the competition.

Ballesteros, on the other hand, had set off a firestorm of controversy for the way Miguel Angel Martin, his own countryman, had been treated after suffering a wrist injury that required surgery following the British Open. Martin, who had qualified on points as the 10th man on the team, was taken off the European side three weeks before the start of the competition, allowing Olazabal to make the team on points and Faldo and Parnevik to be the Captain's choices. As it turned out, Martin couldn't have played anyway, admitting two days before the Matches he was not physically fit enough to compete.

All of that was mostly forgotten when play began on Friday following a morning downpour. By the time darkness halted play, the U.S. and European Teams each won three matches on a day that was equal parts fabulous and frustration for both sides.

Because of an hour-and-40-minute rain and lightning delay, two of the afternoon foursome (alternate shot) matches were not completed when play was suspended at 8:20 p.m. At that point, Americans Tom Lehman and Phil Mickelson were even with Parnevik and Garrido after 12 holes, and Europeans Faldo and Westwood were 2 up after 15 holes, with a good chance to close out the match at the 16th green.

"Isn't the Ryder Cup neat?," Kite said at the end of play. "I'm having a ball out there. This is really exciting. And the so-called experts who said it would be a blowout were proven wrong. This is unbelievably close."

No player on either side was able to be a part of two victories the opening day, but there were plenty of heroes on both teams. Americans Woods and steadying influence Mark O'Meara teamed to beat Montgomerie and Langer by the largest margin of the morning four-ball (best-ball) matches, 3 and 2.

In the afternoon, Langer and Montgomerie, who had said before the Matches that the tight Valderrama course was not suited to Woods' long-ball game, returned the favor. Their 5-and-3 victory over O'Meara and Woods, who was clearly struggling on greens all day, was the most lopsided result of the day.

"I've just got to hit some putts on the (practice) green and get a feel for it," Woods said following his afternoon round. "The rain coming down this morning really screwed up my feel for the greens. They were a little sticky ... When you have big breaking putts, it's hard."

Brad Faxon did not have that problem when it counted the most in the morning round. He had missed a crucial seven-footer that contributed to the Americans' loss two years ago at Oak Hill.

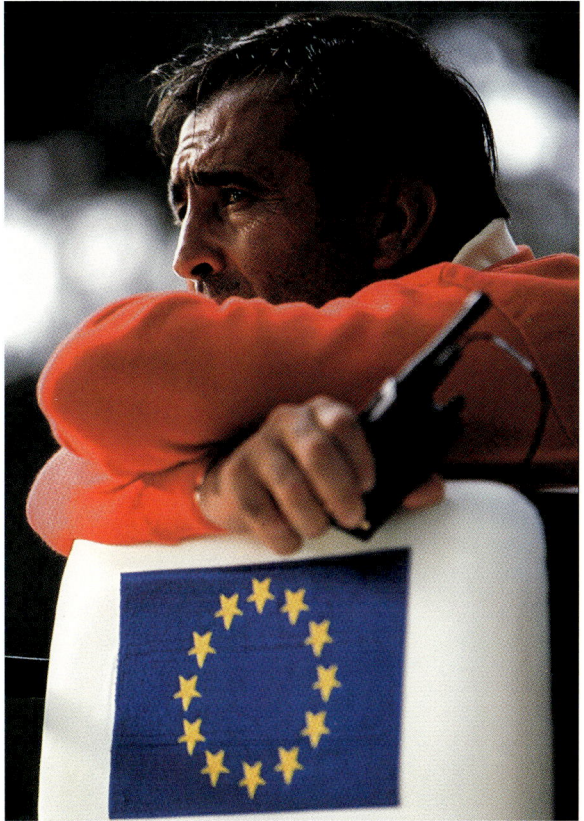

Seve Ballesteros was a fiery European leader.

Bernhard Langer scored in the afternoon play.

Ignacio Garrido (left) delighted his Captain with a halve.

No wonder he got such huge satisfaction from making almost the exact same length putt at the 18th green to halve the hole and save a 1-up victory for himself and Fred Couples over the formidable Faldo and Westwood.

"I got lucky, I got to watch Nick putt first," Faxon said of his match-winning save of par out of a greenside bunker after reading Faldo's line. "I was thinking about Oak Hill. I just said, 'Hit it in the middle of the hole and let's get outta here.' … This was pretty big. I waited two years to have something like that (putt) again."

Only seconds before, Faldo had missed virtually the same putt, from eight feet on the exact line, for a birdie that would have halved the match for his team.

In Faldo and Westwood's afternoon alternate shot match against Leonard and Jeff Maggert, Westwood had a 10-footer for birdie at the 16th that would have clinched a victory. It was so dark, Maggert told the match referee that he did not want to continue playing. Under the rules, any player on either team can call a halt to play if they feel there's not enough light. Faldo and Westwood wanted to finish, but the players marked their golf balls and had to come back at 9 a.m. to finish.

"Jeff did it on his own," Kite said afterward of Maggert's controversial decision to stop play. "As soon as they walked up to the green, Jeff came up to me and said, 'I could barely see the (second) shot I hit (into the 16th green).' I told him if that was the case, he didn't have to play. It was a crucial putt for us, too. I wouldn't have wanted them to have to read the green without being able to see the right line."

Ironically, Lehman and Mickelson wanted to keep playing in a match that was all square after 12 holes. This time, Parnevik, who made two crucial birdie putts paired with fellow Swede Per-Ulrik Johansson to help win his morning match 1 up against Lehman and Furyk, asked that play be stopped for darkness.

There was plenty of light Friday night for Hoch. Playing with Janzen in the alternate shot format, Hoch, a 40-year-old rookie, made an eight-footer on the 18th green for the Americans' final point of the day. That stroke, from a man who missed from less than three feet in a playoff that would have won the 1989 Masters, provided the American side's only afternoon point against home-country hero Olazabal and Italy's Costantino Rocca in a 1-up victory.

"He (Janzen) hit a great iron shot into the (18th) green," said Hoch. "I just told him, 'Lee, read the putt and I'll make it.' I wasn't reading them that well. He read it left center, and I putted it in."

Olazabal and Rocca also had teamed in the morning round for a stirring, and somewhat startling, 1-up victory over Mickelson and Love. Stirring because the Americans were playing well and had a 2-up lead through 11 holes. Startling because Olazabal holed a pitching wedge from 131

Both teams had great spectator support.

yards out in the fairway for an eagle that leveled the match at the 370-yard 14th hole, and Rocca made a four-footer at the 422-yard 16th for birdie and a 1-up advantage.

They took that lead into the last hole, but the Americans had a wonderful chance to halve the match. Mickelson, one of the best putters in the game, had a six-footer for birdie that didn't break the way he had thought. It rolled by the left edge by an agonizing inch to allow the Europeans to celebrate their good fortune with a very precious point.

"The only positive was that at least I was able to put myself in position to halve the match," Mickelson said of his first ever loss in Ryder Cup competition, after going 3-0 at Oak Hill. "That's what I enjoy about competitive golf, getting in position to win. I'm disappointed to miss ... Faldo had the same putt and he missed his right. I missed mine left. I thought it was a right edge putt."

Parnevik, the Swede who had narrowly lost two British Opens in the last four years, had few doubts about his two stunning birdie putts on the 17th and 18th holes in the morning round. Wearing a conventional pair of pants provided by his team instead of those stove-pipe trousers he's usually got on, Parnevik gave his team a 1-up advantage at the 17th with his 15-foot birdie putt at the 511-yard hole.

At the 434-yard 18th, both Lehman and Furyk had second shots to within 12 feet of the pin, but never had a chance to make them. Johansson barely missed his own 15-footer for birdie, and Parnevik spent quite a few seconds studying his own. His attempt was never in doubt and he pumped his fist with great joy, soon accepting a hug from Ballesteros, who was everywhere on the golf course, whooshing around on what seemed to be a jet-propelled golf cart.

"I reckon it was about 18 feet with a two-cup break from right to left," Parnevik said later. "It was a great feeling to see the ball go in and win my first Ryder Cup point."

On Saturday, not a single American player or spectator on the premises — including basketball great Michael Jordan, in from Monaco for the day — had any sort of great feelings. You could see it in the players' and their wives' weary faces at day's end, those looks of abject red, white and very blue dejection. On the second day of the competition, the U.S. Team often played the doomed bull to Europe's all-conquering matador.

Ballesteros' European Team took firm control in defense of the Ryder Cup during Saturday's surprising slaughter, posting three victories and a tie in the morning four-ball (best-ball) matches, after also securing a victory and another tie in the completion of Friday's two foursome (alternate shot) contests.

Led by the iron-willed Faldo and fellow Englishman Westwood — his white-hot rookie partner — with major contributions from four other first-time players, the European side held a sub-

Colin Montgomerie (above) and Darren Clarke started the Europeans' surge on Saturday.

Lee Westwood (left) took direction from Nick Faldo in their Saturday win over O'Meara and Woods.

stantial 9-4 advantage after the first 13 matches of this rain-plagued event.

"It looks like you all are shell-shocked too," Kite said at a news conference filled mostly with U.S. media Saturday night. "It's not insurmountable. We have to play like crazy, but it's not insurmountable. If we're going to get back into the Ryder Cup, something has to happen tomorrow (Sunday) morning."

Because of thunderstorms causing a another two-hour delay, three of the four Saturday afternoon alternate shot matches could not be completed again before darkness closed in.

It began badly for the Americans right from the start of play on Saturday, when Leonard, who played so well with so little success, missed a 20-foot putt for birdie at the 16th hole. Up stepped Westwood and promptly put his 10-footer in the middle of the cup for a birdie that clinched a 3-and-2 victory over Leonard and Maggert to complete Friday's alternate shot match with Faldo.

Tom Lehman (left) shook hands with Olazabal Saturday morning after a halve for the only American point.

Langer (above) and Montgomerie won two foursomes.

After sitting out, Ian Woosnam was ready.

For Faldo, already playing in a record 11th Ryder Cup, it was his 22nd victory, tying a record set by Arnold Palmer in six competitions. Later in the day, still paired with Westwood, his partner in every match over the first two days, Faldo took the record outright with a 2-and-1 victory over still-struggling Woods and O'Meara in their morning foursomes match.

"It was always a goal," Faldo said. "I didn't realize it until Sunday. I was thumbing through a program and saw it and said 'Wow!' The Ryder Cup has been a big part of my life."

When someone asked him about Westwood, his 24-year-old partner, Faldo added, "He's doing all right, just leave him alone."

All the Europeans were doing more than all right. The three players Ballesteros held out in Friday's matches all produced victories Saturday. Welshman Woosnam paired with Denmark's Bjorn for a 2-and-1 victory over Leonard and Faxon in another morning four-ball, and Clarke of Northern Ireland played a major role with Montgomerie in securing a 1-up victory over Couples and Love after going 2 down through 10 holes.

Like Faldo, Montgomerie was a part of two winning points, teaming with Langer to beat Janzen and Furyk 1-up in almost total darkness in the only afternoon alternate shot match completed. Some questioned the wisdom of Janzen attempting and badly missing a 40-foot birdie putt in near darkness, but Kite said the Americans were just trying to do something, anything to stem the European tide.

Earlier in the day, more than 10,000 spectators watched Montgomerie and Clarke take a 1-up lead at Ballesteros' quirky 511-yard 17th. It was here that the European rout began to gain momentum.

Montgomerie hit his tee shot in the right rough and decided to lay up after Clarke hit his second shot into the pond fronting the green. Both Love and Couples hit second shots over the green, but faced extremely difficult approaches to a precarious pin position not far from a slope down to the water.

Now it was Monty's turn, and he did not disappoint the highly partisan European crowd. His third-shot wedge landed about 14 feet above the hole, then slowly began to roll back down the slope toward the pin, with Clarke waving his arm and urging it on every roll of the way. It stopped eight feet short. Couples and Love weren't even close on their third shots, and when Montgomerie holed his birdie putt, the ground shook with a roar heard halfway to Morocco, just across the sea and visible on a clear day.

The drama continued at the 18th, but this time it was Clarke who contributed, hitting his second shot to eight feet but never having to putt after the Americans graciously conceded when their own birdie efforts — Couples missing out of a bunker and Love off line on a 20-foot putt — failed to go in the hole.

American highlights were few and far between. Early in the match, Couples holed a 76-yard pitching wedge for eagle at the 345-yard eighth; Leonard holed an 88-yard sand wedge for eagle at the 535-yard fourth, and Woods chipped in from the fringe for a birdie at the 461-yard seventh, accompanied by a quadruple fist pump.

But the Europeans were far more steady where it counted most, on Valderrama's undulating greens, where their familiarity with slopes and subtle breaks clearly was an advantage.

Still, the Americans weren't ready to give up.

"So far, from what I've seen, there hasn't been one guy that's played well from start to finish," Lehman insisted. "For that reason, I think these guys can be had ... If you can play steady golf through 18 holes, you can take these guys down. I like our chances in singles."

By the time those singles matches began, the Europeans held a commanding 10½-to-5½ lead, and no team in the history of the Ryder Cup had ever come from that far behind to win. In fact, no

Scott Hoch (above) and Jeff Maggert were America's only Saturday winners in the afternoon foursomes.

Rocca (left) and Olazabal closed out a 5-and-4 foursomes win over Fred Couples and Davis Love III.

Young stars Justin Leonard (left) and Woods together got a halve for the Americans on the mostly bleak Saturday.

team had ever come back from more than a two-point deficit to win Samuel Ryder's trophy.

The U.S. went into singles knowing they had to win nine of the 12 matches to bring the Ryder Cup back across the ocean. The Europeans needed only 3½ points to get to 14, the magic number for a tie that would keep the Ryder Cup in Europe.

Kite stacked his lineup appropriately, sending out what he considered to be his five best players at the start — Couples, Love, Woods, Leonard and Mickelson — in an effort to get some momentum, and, best-case scenario, win all five and get to 10½ points to make the Europeans sweat just a touch.

Couples, off first against Woosnam, surely did his part, erupting with five birdies, one eagle and five pars in 11 holes to overwhelm the Welshman, 8 and 7, tying the Ryder Cup record for biggest margin in singles, held by Kite in a victory over Howard Clark in 1989.

Love, off second against Johansson, fought for his life through 12 holes, where the match was even. Johansson won the 13th, 14th and 15th and posted a 3-and-2 win that pushed Europe's lead to 11½ to 6½.

But who could know that Woods, the only American to play in all five matches, would wind up getting beaten by Rocca, 4 and 2, in a match that was over almost before it began. The Italian won three of the first five holes, was 4 up at the turn and coasted home with a 4-and-2 victory. Woods finished the Ryder Cup with a 1-4 record and said later it had been the most nerve-rattling experience of his life.

Rocca got it to 12½ points for Europe with his victory over Woods, and Bjorn somehow managed to overcome losing the first four holes to Leonard to get even through 10 holes. Bjorn birdied the 17th for a 1-up lead, but Leonard made an eight-footer for par that won the 18th and halved the match. Now, the Europeans had 13 points to the

Fred Couples gave the U.S. a singles boost.

Johansson battled back to win the second match.

Rocca (left) shocked Woods with a 4-and-2 win.

Thomas Bjorn (left) halved with Leonard.

Americans' 7, and needed only a victory or two ties in the final eight matches still on the course.

They had to wait awhile to get it. Mickelson chipped in for two eagles on No. 4 and No. 11, both par-fives, and beat Clarke, 2 and 1. And O'Meara shot a front-nine 30 and was seven under par in his 5-and-4 victory over Parnevik, clearly drained from the first two days of play.

For a while on Sunday, it looked as if Olazabal would be the man to keep the Ryder Cup for Europe, a wonderful story if it had played out that way. Ollie had missed 18 months until a comeback earlier in the year from foot problems that actually were caused by a back injury. There were times he even thought he would never play again. Olazabal was 2 up after 15 holes against Janzen, but in a dramatic finish, the American won the last three holes, taking a 1-up triumph when he hit a seven iron to five feet and made the birdie at 18.

Thus, it was left to Langer, the 40-year-old German whose miss of a six-foot putt cost his team the Ryder Cup at Kiawah Island in 1991, to close out Faxon, 2 and 1, on the 17th hole and finally secure the clinching 14th point.

Langer, 2 up at the time, missed this six-footer for birdie, too, at the 17th, but the hole was tied when Faxon couldn't make birdie from 12 feet and lost the match. The denouement touched off spirited celebration all around the green of a treacherous 511-yard hole that was pivotal in a number of matches all week.

"Every Ryder Cup is special in its way," Langer said. "In Kiawah, I was the one who lost the Cup, if you want to say it that way. And this week, I was in the position to make the point ... But this is not an individual event, it's a team event."

Still, not until Montgomerie graciously conceded Hoch's 20-foot par putt at the 18th, allowing their match — the last one still on the course — to end all square, could Europe claim total victory at Valderrama. That final match, played in a torrent of rain, gave both teams one-half point for a tie and put Ballesteros' 12 men over the top.

The Americans had actually gotten to within a point of tying the matches. When Jim Furyk beat Faldo, 3 and 2, Maggert posted a 3-and-2 win

Phil Mickelson chipped in for eagles at No. 4 and here at No. 11 to beat Darren Clarke 2 and 1.

over Westwood, and Lehman, in the anchor spot, dusted Garrido, 7 and 6, it was all up to Monty.

With the match all square through 17 holes, he hit the middle of the fairway off the tee, then the middle of the green to a huge roar from the crowd. Hoch drove from right rough to left rough and was on in three. When Montgomerie's 20-footer for birdie stopped inches from the hole, Hoch conceded his putt, and Montgomerie, eschewing a full point for sportsmanship, did likewise.

Later, in the closing ceremonies shortened because of the continuing deluge, fans huddling under umbrellas nevertheless chanted, "Seve, Seve" and "olé, olé" to honor the European Captain. Said Garrido, "It was our hands on the club, but he hit the shots."

When the Americans look back, they can point to the bleak performances by three of their finest players as a significant reason for the team's fifth loss or tie in the last seven competitions. Woods, Love and Leonard, winner of three of the four majors this year, had a combined Ryder Cup record of one victory, nine losses and three ties.

Lee Janzen won the last three holes against Olazabal.

Langer (right) closed out Faxon to clinch at least a tie.

Montgomerie and Hoch conceded putts, and the victory.

"Hey, these guys are good," said Leonard, who was 0-2-2. "They were playing on a golf course they played quite a bit. They had a big advantage."

The 17th hole also was a killer for the U.S. side. It was there, for example, that Woods hit a 35-foot downhill putt a touch too hard Saturday, only to watch it gather speed and roll all the way down the bank and into the water in a four-ball loss to Westwood and Faldo. It was also there that Langer clinched his singles match and the 14th point.

"That hole has been the difference," Hoch said after Saturday's play.

Kite, whose 12 players were 31 under par in earning eight of 12 singles points on Sunday, said his only regret as Captain was that more of them had not come over to play a course most had never seen. Only Woods, Love and O'Meara visited before the British Open at Royal Troon, although Couples had played there before in the Volvo Masters.

"I have no regrets and no second guessing of anything I did with the possible exception of not being a little stronger in my request to guys to come to Valderrama," Kite said. "I did not get enough of them here. That was a big difference in the match. My guys played better tee to green. But their team chipped better and putted better, not because they were better putters or chippers, but because they knew the golf course.

"We're all very disappointed. I guess, had we played poorly and been blown out, it would have been easier. To play as well as we did and perform as admirably as we did, makes it difficult. We thought we could win the Matches today, and we came up a little short."

Ballesteros clearly had no regrets. Lehman said Ballesteros "kept vaporizing into places" to help his men whenever he could. Never mind that some complained a bit about him offering too much advice, or suggesting shots that only the

Despite a rousing performance on Sunday in the singles, the Americans had less to cheer than the Europeans.

great Seve could have managed out of the trees or equally impossible lies.

When it was over, Ballesteros said that while it may have seemed at times he was flying by the seat of his pants, he really did have a "grand plan" all along.

"Nothing was improvised. I only improvise myself when I am playing in the trees," he said. He also indicated that each of his players was asked to give him two men they would feel comfortable playing with before he made a pairing. He also asked his best players to tell him if they could not play five matches. Both Langer and Rocca said four was enough.

For Ballesteros, age 40, one captaincy is also enough for now. He will try to get back his playing form after several years of dreadful results and back pain. He also wants to make the European Team again in 1999, and perhaps two more after that. For the Ryder Cup's sake, you have to hope it will happen exactly the way he would like.

As Kite said to his friend and long-time foe afterward, "Well done, Seve, well done." Well done, indeed, teardrops or not.

In the end, Ballesteros had a bubbly toast.

32nd Ryder Cup Matches

September 26-28, 1997, Valderrama Golf Club, Sotogrande, Spain

HOLE	1	2	3	4	5	6	7	8	9	10	11	12	13	14	15	16	17	18
PAR	4	4	3	5	4	3	4	4	4	4	4	5	3	4	4	3	4	5	4

FIRST DAY
Morning Fourball

Jose Maria Olazabal and Costantino Rocca (Europe) defeated Davis Love III and Phil Mickelson (USA), 1 up

	1	2	3	4	5	6	7	8	9	10	11	12	13	14	15	16	17	18
Olazabal				5	4	3	4			4	5	3		2			4	4
Rocca		4	2					4	4				3		3		3	
Love	3		3	5	4			4					4	C			4	4
Mickelson		4				3	4		4	3	4	3			3			

Fred Couples and Brad Faxon (USA) defeated Nick Faldo and Lee Westwood (Europe), 1 up

	1	2	3	4	5	6	7	8	9	10	11	12	13	14	15	16	17	18
Faldo				5	4		4	4	3	4	6	3	4	4	4	4	4	4
Westwood	4	3	2		3													
Couples	4	3	3		4		3	4	3	4	5	3				3	4	4
Faxon				5		3							4	4				4

Jesper Parnevik and Per-Ulrik Johansson (Europe) defeated Tom Lehman and Jim Furyk (USA), 1 up

	1	2	3	4	5	6	7	8	9	10	11	12	13	14	15	16	17	18
Parnevik		4	3	4	4							3	5	3		4	4	3
Johansson	4					2		3	4						3	3		
Lehman	3		2	4	4			5	3		3	4	4	2		5		
Furyk				4		3	4	4		5					3			3

Tiger Woods and Mark O'Meara (USA) defeated Colin Montgomerie and Bernhard Langer (Europe), 3 and 2

	1	2	3	4	5	6	7	8	9	10	11	12	13	14	15	16
Montgomerie					5			4			5	3				
Langer	4	4	3	4		4	4		4	4				4	3	3
Woods						4			3						3	
O'Meara	4	4	3		4	3		4			5	3	5	3		3

POINTS: Europe 2, United States 2

Afternoon Foursomes

Scott Hoch and Lee Janzen (USA) defeated Costantino Rocca and Jose Maria Olazabal (Europe), 1 up

	1	2	3	4	5	6	7	8	9	10	11	12	13	14	15	16	17	18
Rocca/Olazabal	4	4	3	5	5	3	3	5	5	4	6	W	5	4	3	4	4	4
Hoch/Janzen	3	3	3	6	5	4	4	4	4	5	C		4	4	3	5	5	3

Nick Faldo and Lee Westwood (Europe) defeated Justin Leonard and Jeff Maggert (USA), 3 and 2

	1	2	3	4	5	6	7	8	9	10	11	12	13	14	15	16
Faldo/Westwood	3	5	3	4	C	3	4	3	4	C	4	3	4	4	3	3
Leonard/Maggert	4	4	2	5	W	3	5	4	5	3	5	2	5	4	3	4

Jesper Parnevik and Ignacio Garrido (Europe) halved with Tom Lehman and Phil Mickelson (USA)

	1	2	3	4	5	6	7	8	9	10	11	12	13	14	15	16	17	18
Parnevik/Garrido	4	4	4	6	4	3	5	3	4	4	5	3	4	3	3	4	5	4
Lehman/Mickelson	4	4	4	4	4	3	4	4	4	5	4	3	4	3	4	4	5	4

Bernhard Langer and Colin Montgomerie (Europe) defeated Mark O'Meara and Tiger Woods (USA), 5 and 3

	1	2	3	4	5	6	7	8	9	10	11	12	13	14	15
Langer/Montgomerie	4	4	2	C	4	3	5	3	3	4	4	3	4	4	2
O'Meara/Woods	4	5	3	4	4	3	5	4	4	4	3	4	5	3	

POINTS: Europe 4½, United States 3½

SECOND DAY
Morning Fourball

Colin Montgomerie and Darren Clarke (Europe) defeated Fred Couples and Davis Love III (USA), 1 up

	1	2	3	4	5	6	7	8	9	10	11	12	13	14	15	16	17	18
Montgomerie	4			5	3	3	4	C	4	4			2			3	4	4
Clarke		4	3								4			5	3	3		
Couples	4					4	2	4	3	5	3		4		3		3	5
Love			4	3	4	4	3						4		3			4

Ian Woosnam and Thomas Bjorn (Europe) defeated Justin Leonard and Brad Faxon (USA), 2 and 1

	1	2	3	4	5	6	7	8	9	10	11	12	13	14	15	16	17
Woosnam					3		3	2			4			3	4	2	
Bjorn	4	4		C			4	3		3		3			4		4	4
Leonard						3	3	2	4		3		3		3	5	4	3	4	4
Faxon	4	4	3					4		5								

Nick Faldo and Lee Westwood (Europe) defeated Tiger Woods and Mark O'Meara (USA), 2 and 1

	1	2	3	4	5	6	7	8	9	10	11	12	13	14	15	16	17
Faldo	4		3		3	4	3						4	4		3	4
Westwood		4		5	3			3	3	4	3				2		
Woods	4		3		3			4	4				4	4	3	4	
O'Meara		4		4		3			3			3					4

80

32ND RYDER CUP MATCHES

Jose Maria Olazabal and Ignacio Garrido (Europe) halved with Phil Mickelson and Tom Lehman (USA)

Player	1	2	3	4	5	6	7	8	9	10	11	12	13	14	15	16	17	18
Olazabal			3		5		3	3			4	5	3				3	4
Garrido	4		2	4			4	4		4				4	3	3		4
Mickelson				4	4				4		3					3	4	4
Lehman	4	3	3			3	4		4			4	3	4	4			4

POINTS: Europe 8, United States 4

Afternoon Foursomes

Colin Montgomerie and Bernhard Langer (Europe) defeated Lee Janzen and Jim Furyk (USA), 1 up

Player	1	2	3	4	5	6	7	8	9	10	11	12	13	14	15	16	17	18
Montgomerie/Langer	4	3	3	5	4	3	5	4	3	3	4	3	5	4	3	4	5	5
Janzen/Furyk	3	4	3	6	4	3	5	4	4	3	4	3	5	4	4	3	5	4	5

Scott Hoch and Jeff Maggert (USA) defeated Nick Faldo and Lee Westwood (Europe), 2 and 1

Player	1	2	3	4	5	6	7	8	9	10	11	12	13	14	15	16	17
Faldo/Westwood	4	3	3	5	3	3	5	4	5	4	5	4	4	4	C	4	5
Hoch/Maggert	4	4	3	6	4	2	5	4	4	3	5	3	4	4	2	4	5

Jesper Parnevik and Ignacio Garrido (Europe) halved with Justin Leonard and Tiger Woods (USA)

Player	1	2	3	4	5	6	7	8	9	10	11	12	13	14	15	16	17	18
Parnevik/Garrido	5	4	3	5	4	3	3	4	3	C	5	3	4	4	2	5	5	4
Leonard/Woods	3	4	3	5	4	4	4	4	3	5	3	4	4	3	4	5	4

Jose Maria Olazabal and Costantino Rocca (Europe) defeated Davis Love III and Fred Couples (USA), 5 and 4

Player	1	2	3	4	5	6	7	8	9	10	11	12
Olazabal/Rocca	4	4	3	4	3	3	3	4	3	5	3	3
Love/Couples	4	3	3	4	4	3	4	5	5	5	3	4	3

POINTS: Europe 10½, United States 5½

THIRD DAY
Singles

Fred Couples (USA) defeated Ian Woosnam (Europe), 8 and 7

Player	1	2	3	4	5	6	7	8	9	10	11
Woosnam	5	4	3	4	3	4	4	5			
Couples	4	4	3	3	3	2	4	4	3	3	4

Per-Ulrik Johansson (Europe) defeated Davis Love III (USA), 3 and 2

Player	1	2	3	4	5	6	7	8	9	10	11	12	13	14	15	16
Johansson	4	3	3	5	3	3	6	3	5	4	4	3	4	3	3	4
Love	3	4	3	5	4	3	3	4	5	3	4	3	6	4	4	4

Costantino Rocca (Europe) defeated Tiger Woods (USA), 4 and 2

Player	1	2	3	4	5	6	7	8	9	10	11	12	13	14	15	16
Rocca	3	4	3	5	3	3	4	4	4	5	3	4	4	3	4	
Woods	4	4	4	5	4	3	4	4	5	4	4	3	4	3	5	

Thomas Bjorn (Europe) halved with Justin Leonard (USA)

Player	1	2	3	4	5	6	7	8	9	10	11	12	13	14	15	16	17	18
Bjorn	4	5	3	5	3	3	4	4	3	4	5	3	4	3	4	4	4	5
Leonard	3	4	2	4	4	3	4	5	4	5	4	4	3	5	3	5	5	4

Phil Mickelson (USA) defeated Darren Clarke (Europe), 2 and 1

Player	1	2	3	4	5	6	7	8	9	10	11	12	13	14	15	16	17
Clarke	4	4	4	4	3	3	5	4	3	4	C	3	4	4	3	4	4
Mickelson	4	3	3	3	4	3	5	5	5	4	3	3	4	5	3	3	4

Mark O'Meara (USA) defeated Jesper Parnevik (Europe), 5 and 4

Player	1	2	3	4	5	6	7	8	9	10	11	12
Parnevik	4	4	2	5	5	3	4	4	4	4	3	5	3
O'Meara	4	3	3	4	3	3	3	3	4	4	3	4	3

Lee Janzen (USA) defeated Jose Maria Olazabal (Europe), 1 up

Player	1	2	3	4	5	6	7	8	9	10	11	12	13	14	15	16	17	18
Olazabal	4	4	2	5	4	3	5	4	4	3	5	3	3	4	3	5	5	4
Janzen	4	4	3	5	3	4	4	3	5	4	5	2	4	4	4	4	4	3

Bernhard Langer (Europe) defeated Brad Faxon (USA), 2 and 1

Player	1	2	3	4	5	6	7	8	9	10	11	12	13	14	15	16	17
Langer	4	4	2	5	4	3	4	4	5	4	5	5	4	4	3	4	5
Faxon	4	4	3	5	4	3	5	5	4	3	5	2	5	5	3	4	5

Jeff Maggert (USA) defeated Lee Westwood (Europe), 3 and 2

Player	1	2	3	4	5	6	7	8	9	10	11	12	13	14	15	16
Westwood	4	3	3	4	5	3	4	4	4	3	5	3	3	4	3	3
Maggert	3	3	3	4	5	2	4	4	3	4	4	3	3	4	3	3

Colin Montgomerie (Europe) halved with Scott Hoch (USA)

Player	1	2	3	4	5	6	7	8	9	10	11	12	13	14	15	16	17	18
Montgomerie	4	4	3	5	5	4	3	4	5	3	5	3	4	3	4	3	5	4
Hoch	4	4	3	5	3	3	4	4	5	4	5	3	4	5	3	5	4	4

Jim Furyk (USA) defeated Nick Faldo (Europe), 3 and 2

Player	1	2	3	4	5	6	7	8	9	10	11	12	13	14	15	16
Faldo	3	C	2	5	4	4	4	5	3	5	3	4	3	2	5	
Furyk	4	4	3	5	4	3	4	3	5	3	4	3	4	3	2	4

Tom Lehman (USA) defeated Ignacio Garrido (Europe), 7 and 6

Player	1	2	3	4	5	6	7	8	9	10	11	12
Garrido	4	4	4	5	4	3	5	3	4	2	5	4
Lehman	4	3	3	5	3	2	5	3	3	4	4	3

TOTAL POINTS: Europe 14½, United States 13½

LEGEND: C—conceded hole to opponent; W—won hole by concession without holing out.

RECORDS FALL AS ELS FINDS HIS PARADISE

By Bill Kwon

Tiger Woods drew the crowds and led the first round.

Ernie Els has found his paradise, his Bali Hai. It's the Garden Island of Kauai, where the movie *South Pacific*, featuring the song "Bali Hai," was filmed.

"My only visit to the Hawaiian Islands has been to Kauai," said Els, who loves the island's laid-back lifestyle. He talked about maybe "building a little house" there some day. In two visits, Els has come away with $600,000.

The 28-year-old South African became the champion of champions by winning the 1997 MasterCard PGA Grand Slam in mid-November at the Poipu Bay Resort course, breaking two tournaments records en route to the $400,000 top prize.

Els, who won his second U.S. Open in 1997, shot a final-round 65 for a 36-hole total of 133 to beat Masters champion Tiger Woods by three strokes. In 1994, Els had placed third behind Greg Norman and Nick Price after qualifying for the MasterCard PGA Grand Slam with his first U.S. Open title.

"I'm obviously satisfied with the victory. When you play in the MasterCard PGA Grand Slam,

With a birdie on the final hole, Ernie Els broke the single-round record with 65 and tournament record with a 134 total.

His first-round 77 meant Justin Leonard was destined to place fourth among the year's major championship winners.

Els started with 68 including two late bogeys.

you're going to play against some really good players," Els said.

Els birdied the final hole for his 65 to better the tournament low of 66 set by Norman in 1994 and tied by 1996 champion Tom Lehman. Els also bettered Lehman's 36-hole mark of 134.

Davis Love III, the PGA Champion, finished third at 138, and British Open winner Justin Leonard, never recovering from a poor opening round, was a distant fourth at 149.

While Els captured the title, Woods captivated most of the 6,000 fans, who made up the largest gallery ever to see a golf event on the oldest island in the Hawaiian chain.

Woods, the PGA of America's Player of the Year, led after the first day, shooting a six-under-par 66 despite seeing the course for the first time. He had arrived the day before and had played only the first eight holes and the par-five 18th. He cut short his practice round because of a slight cold.

Els was two strokes back with 68 following back-to-back bogeys at Nos. 15 and 16, while Love posted 71 and Leonard, 77, as a Kona wind, instead of the prevailing trades, made the final four holes more difficult.

Wielding a torrid putter, Els came blistering back with a five-under-par 31 on the first nine in the soggy second round when two inches of rain soaked the course overnight. It left the majority of Poipu Bay's 86 bunkers with standing water. The players were allowed to lift, clean and place their balls.

"I didn't think we were going to play," said Els, who overtook Woods after sinking a four-foot birdie putt at the 25th hole of the tournament — the par-three 152-yard seventh. "Obviously, my putter got red-hot on the front nine. I think my putter was the key."

The only one of the four to have played at Poipu Bay before, Els admitted that it proved an advantage, especially in reading the greens. "I had a pretty good feel of the greens and what to expect this week," said Els, who at 6-foot-3, 210 pounds, looks more like a football linebacker than a world-class golfer.

Els had finished 26th in the 30-player Tour Championship two weeks before the MasterCard PGA Grand Slam. "I didn't play well there, so I probably needed two weeks off," Els said. "Coming here I thought I was a little rusty, but playing the golf course three years ago probably helped me a little bit this week, especially reading the greens."

Making a birdie to start off the second round got Els in the right frame of mind. "The first hole was quite big, I think," he said.

"Ernie got off to a great start and I didn't make the putts early when I had a chance," said Woods. "For a guy that big, he has a nice touch. He has a touch to die for."

Not that Woods doesn't have one also.

Tiger wowed even himself with two shots after taking drops out of water-filled bunkers for a birdie at the par-five 14th and a marvelous par at the 501-yard, par-four 16th. The latter was the shot of the day. His second shot found the right greenside bunker. His first free drop rolled to the edge

Woods cut short his practice because of a cold.

Davis Love III enjoyed Kauai with his son.

Woods' bunker play was spectacular in both rounds, especially his shot on the 16th hole on the second day.

Els was the only one who had played Poipu Bay before.

of a huge puddle, so Woods dropped again. He had a nasty downhill lie. Woods thought of pitching out sideways and two-putting for a bogey.

"I came to the conclusion that in order for me to win the tournament, I had to go right at it," Woods said. His ball flew out low, skidded along the green and stopped three feet from the flagstick, enabling him to save his par.

"Wow. I've got to give myself a hand on that one," Woods said as he climbed out of the waterlogged bunker. "You gotta give me two skins for that one."

As for Love, his opening-round 71 made it difficult to overtake Woods and Els. "I didn't get off to a good start," said Love, referring to his one-over-par play on the first seven holes. "I just hung in there. But, unfortunately, in a two-day event, that's not going to be quite good enough."

It turned out to be true.

He hit two spectators on his drive at the par-five second hole. Love thought inconsistent play was more responsible for his so-so start than what

Birdies on four of the first five holes put Love in contention in the second round, but then his putts stopped falling.

happened on his errant drive. "You always feel pretty bad and lose a little concentration when you hit somebody, whether it's a good shot or a bad shot. And I hit a bad shot," Love said.

He bounced back the next day by birdieing four of his first five holes, including No. 2. But the putts stopped dropping as he missed very makeable birdie tries in the next five holes before birdieing No. 11.

"Ernie had such a good front nine, he kind of kept me out of it," Love said.

"I'm thankful that Tiger and Davis didn't get off on a hot streak," Els said.

"What about me?" asked Leonard, feigning a hurt look.

"You had a hot streak. You made about seven pars in a row there. Not bad," Els replied.

Leonard also got a ribbing from TBS golf commentator David Feherty: "The way he's going, Justin's lucky he doesn't finish fifth. At least he had a top-10 finish."

"Fourth place. I can put that on my resume,"

Leonard shot even-par 72 for his 149 total.

"Obviously, my putter got red-hot on the front nine," Els said. *"I think my putter was the key."*

Leonard said, going along with the good-natured bantering.

"When Ernie made par on the first hole (of the first round), that was as big a lead as he needed on me," Leonard said.

There was no more dramatic effect of the wind change during the two days than at the 537-yard, par-five 14th hole, which normally plays into the wind.

In the first round, with the opposite wind, Woods hit driver and seven iron from 196 yards out to within eight feet of the pin for an eagle. The next day, with a breath of wind in his face, Woods couldn't get there with a three iron from 217 yards away. But he birdied the hole with a great sand shot that saw him with his left leg in the bunker and his right knee on the grassy slope just outside of it.

The wind shift also made Poipu Bay's four finishing holes play differently. "The four holes coming back were pretty tough," said Els.

Tell that to Leonard, especially after his adventures at the 501-yard 16th, which normally is an easy par-four despite its length because of a prevailing tradewind. The fairway is along a cliff overlooking the Pacific Ocean with a lava rock wall on the left.

On the first day, Leonard pulled a three wood on his second shot and it ricocheted off the lava barrier and nestled in the rough about two feet from the wall, restricting his swing. It's more than just a lateral water hazard. Because it's considered a sacred Hawaiian site, the local rule states that a player cannot touch the wall with his stance or club.

"You've got to be kidding," exclaimed Leonard, who elected to punch the ball out sideways. He found the right greenside bunker, blasted out and two-putted for a double-bogey six.

"It was not a fun day," said the young Texan, who parred the hole the next time around. He kept saying *mahalo* (thank you) after each shot.

He wasn't about to offend the Hawaiian gods.

It also didn't help that Leonard was the shortest off the tees compared to the other three long-knockers. "I would pay my way to watch them hit the ball," Leonard said. "I knew I was going to be hitting first on second shots ... third shots ... fourth shots." The fifth shot? "Well, these guys were done by then, so I was the only one left," Leonard added.

The fans, including many youngsters who played hooky from school, got their money's worth watching Tiger. His bunker escapes provided the MasterCard PGA Grand Slam with two of its most memorable shots. But on the first day, Woods' best shot was an eight-footer that he sank for a bogey. That was at the par-four, 384-yard 13th hole when his sand wedge from 95 yards drew back and rolled into a lake guarding the right side of the green.

Hitting a pitching wedge this time after losing stroke and distance, Woods then dropped the putt for his bogey that got his momentum going, resulting in an eagle at No. 14 and birdies at Nos. 16 and 18 for the first-day lead.

A second-round 70, which Woods called "untidy," lost ground to Els' record 65. "I didn't make the putts early when I had chances," Woods said. "I fell behind and Ernie was making everything."

So in the end, in the tournament involving the major champions of 1997, it was all Els.

MasterCard PGA Grand Slam
November 17-18, 1997,
Poipu Bay Resort, Kauai, Hawaii

Contestant	Rounds		Total	Prize
Ernie Els	68	65	133	$400,000
Tiger Woods	66	70	136	250,000
Davis Love III	71	67	138	200,000
Justin Leonard	77	72	149	150,000

PGA Seniors' Championship

Year	Champion	Score	Runners-up	Venue
1937	Jock Hutchison	223	George Gordon	Augusta National GC, Augusta, GA
1938	*Freddie McLeod	154	Otto Hackbarth	Augusta National GC, Augusta, GA
1940	*Otto Hackbarth	146	Jock Hutchison	Bobby Jones GC & North Shore CC, Sarasota, FL
1941	Jack Burke, Sr.	142	Eddie Williams	Bobby Jones GC & Sarasota Bay CC, Sarasota, FL
1942	Eddie Williams	138	George Morris	Fort Myers CC, Fort Myers, FL
1943-44	No Championship — World War II			
1945	Eddie Williams	150	Jock Hutchison	PGA National GC, Dunedin, FL
1946	*Eddie Williams	146	Jock Hutchison	PGA National GC, Dunedin, FL
1947	Jock Hutchison	145	Ben Richter	PGA National GC, Dunedin, FL
1948	Charles McKenna	141	Ben Richter	PGA National GC, Dunedin, FL
1949	Marshall Crichton	145	Lou Chiapetta, George Smith	PGA National GC, Dunedin, FL
1950	Al Watrous	142	Bill Jellife	PGA National GC, Dunedin, FL
1951	*Al Watrous	142	Jock Hutchison	PGA National GC, Dunedin, FL
1952	Ernie Newnham	146	Al Watrous	PGA National GC, Dunedin, FL
1953	Harry Schwab	142	Gene Sarazen, Charles McKenna	PGA National GC, Dunedin, FL
1954	Gene Sarazen	214	Al Watrous, Perry Del Vecchio	PGA National GC, Dunedin, FL
1955	Mortie Dutra	213	Mike Murra, Gene Sarazen, Denny Shute	PGA National GC, Dunedin, FL
1956	Pete Burke	215	Ock Willoweit	PGA National GC, Dunedin, FL
1957	*Al Watrous	210	Bob Stupple	PGA National GC, Dunedin, FL
1958	Gene Sarazen	288	Charles Sheppard	PGA National GC, Dunedin, FL
1959	Willie Goggin	284	Duke Gibson, Paul Runyan, Denny Shute	PGA National GC, Dunedin, FL
1960	Dick Metz	284	Tony Longo, Paul Runyan	PGA National GC, Dunedin, FL
1961	Paul Runyan	278	Jimmy Demaret	PGA National GC, Dunedin, FL
1962	Paul Runyan	278	Errie Ball, Joe Brown, Dutch Harrison	PGA National GC, Dunedin, FL
1963	Herman Barron	272	John Barnum	Port St. Lucie CC, Port St. Lucie, FL
1964	Sam Snead	279	John Barnum	PGA National GC, Palm Beach Gardens, FL
1965	Sam Snead	278	Joe Lopez, Sr.	Fort Lauderdale CC, Fort Lauderdale, FL
1966	Fred Haas, Jr.	286	Dutch Harrison, John Barnum	PGA National GC, Palm Beach Gardens, FL
1967	Sam Snead	279	Bob Hamilton	PGA National GC, Palm Beach Gardens, FL
1968	Chandler Harper	279	Sam Snead	PGA National GC, Palm Beach Gardens, FL
1969	Tommy Bolt	278	Peter Fleming	PGA National GC, Palm Beach Gardens, FL

PREVIOUS RESULTS

Year	Champion	Score	Runners-up	Venue
1970	Sam Snead	290	Fred Haas	PGA National GC, Palm Beach Gardens, FL
1971	Julius Boros	285	Tommy Bolt	PGA National GC, Palm Beach Gardens, FL
1972	Sam Snead	286	Julius Boros, Tommy Bolt	PGA National GC, Palm Beach Gardens, FL
1973	Sam Snead	268	Julius Boros	PGA National GC, Palm Beach Gardens, FL
1974	Roberto de Vicenzo	273	Julius Boros, Art Wall	Port St. Lucie CC, Port St. Lucie, FL
1975	*Charles Sifford	280	Fred Wampler	Walt Disney World, Orlando, FL
1976	Pete Cooper	283	Fred Wampler	Walt Disney World, Orlando, FL
1977	Julius Boros	283	Fred Haas, Jr.	Walt Disney World, Orlando, FL
1978	*Joe Jimenez	286	Manuel de la Torre, Joe Cheves	Walt Disney World, Orlando, FL
1979	*Jack Fleck	289	Bill Johnston, Bob Erickson	Walt Disney World, Orlando, FL
1979	Don January	270	George Bayer	Turnberry Isle CC, North Miami Beach, FL
1980	*Arnold Palmer	289	Paul Harney	Turnberry Isle CC, North Miami Beach, FL
1981	Miller Barber	281	Arnold Palmer	Turnberry Isle CC, North Miami Beach, FL
1982	Don January	288	Julius Boros	PGA National GC, Palm Beach Gardens, FL
1984	Arnold Palmer	282	Don January	PGA National GC, Palm Beach Gardens, FL
1984	Peter Thomson	286	Don January	PGA National GC, Palm Beach Gardens, FL
1986	Gary Player	281	Lee Elder	PGA National GC, Palm Beach Gardens, FL
1987	Chi Chi Rodriguez	282	Dale Douglass	PGA National GC, Palm Beach Gardens, FL
1988	Gary Player	284	Chi Chi Rodriguez	PGA National GC, Palm Beach Gardens, FL
1989	Larry Mowry	281	Miller Barber, Al Geiberger	PGA National GC, Palm Beach Gardens, FL
1990	Gary Player	281	Chi Chi Rodriguez	PGA National GC, Palm Beach Gardens, FL
1991	Jack Nicklaus	271	Bruce Crampton	PGA National GC, Palm Beach Gardens, FL
1992	Lee Trevino	278	Mike Hill	PGA National GC, Palm Beach Gardens, FL
1993	*Tom Wargo	275	Bruce Crampton	PGA National GC, Palm Beach Gardens, FL
1994	Lee Trevino	279	Jim Colbert	PGA National GC, Palm Beach Gardens, FL
1995	Raymond Floyd	277	John Paul Cain, Larry Gilbert, Lee Trevino	PGA National GC, Palm Beach Gardens, FL
1996	Hale Irwin	280	Isao Aoki	PGA National GC, Palm Beach Gardens, FL
1997	Hale Irwin	274	Jack Nicklaus, Dale Douglass	PGA National GC, Palm Beach Gardens, FL

(* Playoff)

PGA Championship

Year	Champion	Score	Runners-up	Venue
1916	James M. Barnes	1-up	Jock Hutchison	Siwanoy CC, Bronxville, New York, NY
1917-18	No Championship — World War I			
1919	James M. Barnes	6 and 5	Fred McLeod	Engineers CC, Roslyn, NY
1920	Jock Hutchison	1-up	J. Douglas Edgar	Flossmoor CC, Flossmoor, IL
1921	Walter Hagen	3 and 2	James M. Barnes	Inwood CC, Far Rockaway, NY
1922	Gene Sarazen	4 and 3	Emmet French	Oakmont CC, Oakmont, PA
1923	Gene Sarazen	38 holes	Walter Hagen	Pelham CC, Pelham Manor, NY
1924	Walter Hagen	2-up	James M. Barnes	French Lick CC, French Lick, IN
1925	Walter Hagen	6 and 5	William Mehlhorn	Olympia Fields CC, Olympia Fields, IL
1926	Walter Hagen	5 and 3	Leo Diegel	Salisbury GC, Westbury, NY
1927	Walter Hagen	1-up	Joe Turnesa	Cedar Crest CC, Dallas, TX
1928	Leo Diegel	6 and 5	Al Espinosa	Five Farms CC, Baltimore, MD
1929	Leo Diegel	6 and 4	Johnny Farrell	Hillcrest CC, Los Angeles, CA
1930	Tommy Armour	1-up	Gene Sarazen	Fresh Meadow CC, Flushing, NY
1931	Tom Creavy	2 and 1	Denny Shute	Wannamoisett CC, Rumford, RI
1932	Olin Dutra	4 and 3	Frank Walsh	Keller GC, St. Paul, MN
1933	Gene Sarazen	5 and 4	Willie Goggin	Blue Mound CC, Milwaukee, WI
1934	Paul Runyan	38 holes	Craig Wood	Park CC, Williamsville, NY
1935	Johnny Revolta	5 and 4	Tommy Armour	Twin Hills CC, Oklahoma City, OK
1936	Denny Shute	3 and 2	Jimmy Thomson	Pinehurst CC, Pinehurst, NC
1937	Denny Shute	37 holes	Harold McSpaden	Pittsburgh FC, Aspinwall, PA
1938	Paul Runyan	8 and 7	Sam Snead	Shawnee CC, Shawnee-On-Delaware, PA
1939	Henry Picard	37 holes	Byron Nelson	Pomonok CC, Flushing, NY
1940	Byron Nelson	1-up	Sam Snead	Hershey CC, Hershey, PA
1941	Vic Ghezzi	38 holes	Byron Nelson	Cherry Hills CC, Denver, CO
1942	Sam Snead	2 and 1	Jim Turnesa	Seaview CC, Atlantic City, NJ
1943	No Championship — World War II			
1944	Bob Hamilton	1-up	Byron Nelson	Manito G and CC, Spokane, WA
1945	Byron Nelson	4 and 3	Sam Byrd	Moraine CC, Dayton, OH
1946	Ben Hogan	6 and 4	Ed Oliver	Portland GC, Portland, OR
1947	Jim Ferrier	2 and 1	Chick Harbert	Plum Hollow CC, Detroit, MI
1948	Ben Hogan	7 and 6	Mike Turnesa	Norwood Hills CC, St. Louis, MO
1949	Sam Snead	3 and 2	Johnny Palmer	Hermitage CC, Richmond, VA
1950	Chandler Harper	4 and 3	Henry Williams, Jr.	Scioto CC, Columbus, OH
1951	Sam Snead	7 and 6	Walter Burkemo	Oakmont CC, Oakmont, PA
1952	Jim Turnesa	1-up	Chick Harbert	Big Spring CC, Louisville, KY
1953	Walter Burkemo	2 and 1	Felice Torza	Birmingham CC, Birmingham, AL
1954	Chick Harbert	4 and 3	Walter Burkemo	Keller GC, St. Paul, MN
1955	Doug Ford	4 and 3	Cary Middlecoff	Meadowbrook CC, Detroit, MI
1956	Jack Burke	3 and 2	Ted Kroll	Blue Hill CC, Boston, MA
1957	Lionel Hebert	2 and 1	Dow Finsterwald	Miami Valley CC, Dayton, OH
1958	Dow Finsterwald	276	Billy Casper	Llanerch CC, Havertown, PA
1959	Bob Rosburg	277	Jerry Barber, Doug Sanders	Minneapolis GC, St. Louis Park, MN

PREVIOUS RESULTS

Year	Champion	Score	Runners-up	Venue
1960	Jay Hebert	281	Jim Ferrier	Firestone CC, Akron, OH
1961	*Jerry Barber	277	Don January	Olympia Fields CC, Olympia Fields, IL
1962	Gary Player	278	Bob Goalby	Aronimink GC, Newtown Square, PA
1963	Jack Nicklaus	279	Dave Ragan, Jr.	Dallas Athletic Club, Dallas, TX
1964	Bobby Nichols	271	Jack Nicklaus, Arnold Palmer	Columbus CC, Columbus, OH
1965	Dave Marr	280	Billy Casper, Jack Nicklaus	Laurel Valley CC, Ligonier, PA
1966	Al Geiberger	280	Dudley Wysong	Firestone CC, Akron, OH
1967	*Don January	281	Don Massengale	Columbine CC, Littleton, CO
1968	Julius Boros	281	Bob Charles, Arnold Palmer	Pecan Valley CC, San Antonio, TX
1969	Raymond Floyd	276	Gary Player	NCR CC, Dayton, OH
1970	Dave Stockton	279	Arnold Palmer, Bob Murphy	Southern Hills CC, Tulsa, OK
1971	Jack Nicklaus	281	Billy Casper	PGA National GC, Palm Beach Gardens, FL
1972	Gary Player	281	Tommy Aaron	Oakland Hills CC, Birmingham, MI
1973	Jack Nicklaus	277	Bruce Crampton	Canterbury GC, Cleveland, OH
1974	Lee Trevino	276	Jack Nicklaus	Tanglewood GC, Winston-Salem, NC
1975	Jack Nicklaus	276	Bruce Crampton	Firestone CC, Akron, OH
1976	Dave Stockton	281	Raymond Floyd, Don January	Congressional CC, Bethesda, MD
1977	*Lanny Wadkins	282	Gene Littler	Pebble Beach GL, Pebble Beach, CA
1978	*John Mahaffey	276	Jerry Pate, Tom Watson	Oakmont CC, Oakmont, PA
1979	*David Graham	272	Ben Crenshaw	Oakland Hills CC, Birmingham, MI
1980	Jack Nicklaus	274	Andy Bean	Oak Hill CC, Rochester, NY
1981	Larry Nelson	273	Fuzzy Zoeller	Atlanta Athletic Club, Duluth, GA
1982	Raymond Floyd	272	Lanny Wadkins	Southern Hills CC, Tulsa, OK
1983	Hal Sutton	274	Jack Nicklaus	Riviera CC, Pacific Palisades, CA
1984	Lee Trevino	273	Lanny Wadkins, Gary Player	Shoal Creek CC, Birmingham, AL
1985	Hubert Green	278	Lee Trevino	Cherry Hills CC, Denver, CO
1986	Bob Tway	276	Greg Norman	Inverness Club, Toledo, OH
1987	*Larry Nelson	287	Lanny Wadkins	PGA National GC, Palm Beach Gardens, FL
1988	Jeff Sluman	272	Paul Azinger	Oak Tree GC, Edmond, OK
1989	Payne Stewart	276	Andy Bean, Mike Reid, Curtis Strange	Kemper Lakes GC, Hawthorn Woods, IL
1990	Wayne Grady	282	Fred Couples	Shoal Creek CC, Birmingham, AL
1991	John Daly	276	Bruce Lietzke	Crooked Stick GC, Carmel, IN
1992	Nick Price	278	John Cook, Nick Faldo, Jim Gallagher, Jr., Gene Sauers	Bellerive CC, St. Louis, MO
1993	*Paul Azinger	272	Greg Norman	Inverness Club, Toledo, OH
1994	Nick Price	269	Corey Pavin	Southern Hills CC, Tulsa, OK
1995	*Steve Elkington	267	Colin Montgomerie	Riviera CC, Pacific Palisades, CA
1996	*Mark Brooks	277	Kenny Perry	Valhalla GC, Louisville, KY
1997	Davis Love III	269	Justin Leonard	Winged Foot GC, Mamaroneck, NY

(* Playoff)

Ryder Cup Matches

Year	Venue	Results			
1927	Worcester CC, Worcester, MA	U.S.	9½	Britain	2½
1929	Moortown GC, Leeds, England	Britain	7	U.S.	5
1931	Scioto CC, Columbus, OH	U.S.	9	Britain	3
1933	Southport & Ainsdale GC, Southport, England	Britain	6½	U.S.	5½
1935	Ridgewood CC, Ridgewood, NJ	U.S.	9	Britain	3
1937	Southport & Ainsdale GC, Southport, England	U.S.	8	Britain	4
1939-1945	No Matches — World War II				
1947	Portland GC, Portland, OR	U.S.	11	Britain	1
1949	Ganton GC, Scarborough, England	U.S.	7	Britain	5
1951	Pinehurst CC, Pinehurst, NC	U.S.	9½	Britain	2½
1953	Wentworth GC, Wentworth, England	U.S.	6½	Britain	5½
1955	Thunderbird CC, Palm Springs, CA	U.S.	8	Britain	4
1957	Lindrick GC, Yorkshire, England	Britain	7½	U.S.	4½
1959	Eldorado CC, Palm Desert, CA	U.S.	8½	Britain	3½
1961	Royal Lytham & St. Annes, St. Annes, England	U.S.	14½	Britain	9½
1963	East Lake CC, Atlanta, GA	U.S.	23	Britain	9
1965	Royal Birkdale GC, Southport, England	U.S.	19½	Britain	12½
1967	Champions GC, Houston, TX	U.S.	23½	Britain	8½
1969	Royal Birkdale GC, Southport, England	U.S.	16	Britain	16
1971	Old Warson CC, St. Louis, MO	U.S.	18½	Britain	13½
1973	Muirfield, Scotland	U.S.	19	G.B. & I.	13
1975	Laurel Valley GC, Ligonier, PA	U.S.	21	G.B. & I.	11
1977	Royal Lytham & St. Annes, St. Annes, England	U.S.	12½	G.B. & I.	7½
1979	The Greenbrier, White Sulphur Springs, WV	U.S.	17	Europe	11
1981	Walton Health GC, Surrey, England	U.S.	18½	Europe	9½
1983	PGA National GC, Palm Beach Gardens, FL	U.S.	14½	Europe	13½
1985	The Belfry, Sutton Coldfield, England	Europe	16½	U.S.	11½
1987	Muirfield Village GC, Dublin, OH	Europe	15	U.S.	13
1989	The Belfry, Sutton Coldfield, England	Europe	14	U.S.	14
1991	The Ocean Course, Kiawah Island, SC	U.S.	14½	Europe	13½
1993	The Belfry, Sutton Coldfield, England	U.S.	15	Europe	13
1995	Oak Hill CC, Rochester, NY	Europe	14½	U.S.	13½
1997	Valderrama GC, Sotogrande, Spain	Europe	14½	U.S.	13½

PGA Grand Slam

Year	Venue	Contestants (Scores)
1979	Oak Hill CC, Rochester, NY	Gary Player (73), Andy North (73), Jack Nicklaus (77), John Mahaffey (77)
1980	Hazeltine National GC, Chaska, MN	Lanny Wadkins (71), Hale Irwin (73), David Graham (74), Fuzzy Zoeller (74)
1981	Breakers West GC, West Palm Beach, FL	Lee Trevino (68), Tom Watson (71), Jack Nicklaus (72), Seve Ballesteros (75)
1982	PGA National, Palm Beach Gardens, FL	Bill Rogers (71), David Graham (76), Larry Nelson (77), Tom Watson (78)
1986	Kemper Lakes GC, Hawthorn Woods, IL	Greg Norman (70), Fuzzy Zoeller (72), Jack Nicklaus (75), Bob Tway (75)
1988	Kemper Lakes GC, Hawthorn Woods, IL	Larry Nelson (69), Larry Mize (70), Scott Simpson (70), Greg Norman (73)
1989	Kemper Lakes GC, Hawthorn Woods, IL	Curtis Strange (73), Craig Stadler (75), Ian Baker-Finch (76), Greg Norman (No Score)
1990	Kemper Lakes GC, Hawthorn Woods, IL	Andy North (70), Craig Stadler (74), Payne Stewart (75), Curtis Strange (WD)
1991	Kauai Lagoons Resort, Kauai, HI	Ian Woosnam (69-66-135), Ian Baker-Finch (68-71-139), Payne Stewart (70-71-141), John Daly (73-70-143)
1992	PGA West, La Quinta, CA	*Nick Price (70-67-137), Tom Kite (75-62-137), Fred Couples (71-71-142) Nick Faldo (72-71-143)
1993	PGA West, La Quinta, CA	Greg Norman (71-74-145), Paul Azinger (75-72-147), Lee Janzen (74-74-148) Bernhard Langer (78-70-148)
1994	Poipu Bay Resort, Kauai, HI	Greg Norman (70-66-136), Nick Price (70-69-139), Ernie Els (72-71-143), Jose Maria Olazabal (74-70-144)
1995	Poipu Bay Resort, Kauai, HI	Ben Crenshaw (72-68-140), Steve Elkington (71-70-141), Corey Pavin (71-70-141), John Daly (75-73-148)
1996	Poipu Bay Resort, Kauai, HI	Tom Lehman (68-66-134), Steve Jones (70-66-136), Nick Faldo (67-72-139), Mark Brooks (74-73-147)
1997	Poipu Bay Resort, Kauai, HI	Ernie Els (68-65-133), Tiger Woods (66-70-136), Davis Love III (71-67-138), Justin Leonard (77-72-149)

(* Playoff)

PGA NATIONAL RESORT & SPA
Palm Beach Gardens, Florida

Hole	Par	Yardage	Hole	Par	Yardage
1	4	346	10	5	549
2	4	419	11	4	412
3	5	539	12	4	397
4	4	355	13	4	370
5	3	171	14	4	422
6	5	478	15	3	164
7	3	185	16	4	412
8	4	422	17	3	152
9	4	381	18	5	528
	36	3,296		36	3,406
				72	6,702

POIPU BAY RESORT GOLF COURSE
Koloa, Kauai, Hawaii

Hole	Par	Yardage	Hole	Par	Yardage
1	4	428	10	4	394
2	5	524	11	3	193
3	3	209	12	4	412
4	4	380	13	4	384
5	4	355	14	5	537
6	5	573	15	4	427
7	3	152	16	4	501
8	4	334	17	3	201
9	4	405	18	5	550
	36	3,360		36	3,599
				72	6,959